The Deceptively Easy
DESSERT COOKBOOK

The Deceptively Easy

DESSERT

❧ COOKBOOK ❧

Simple Recipes for Extraordinary
No-Bake & Baked Sweets

ROBIN DONOVAN

ROCKRIDGE
PRESS

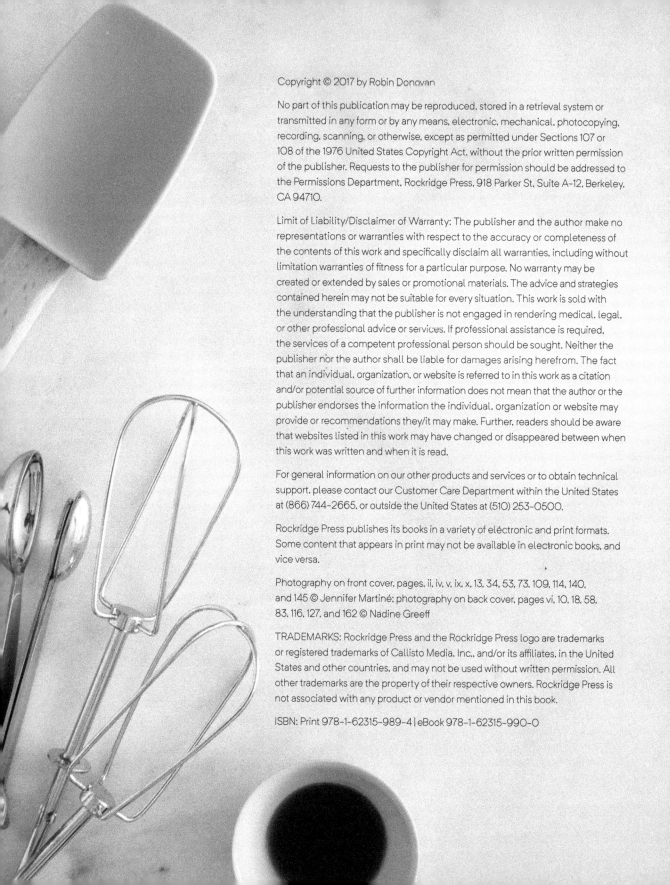

For general information on our other products and services or to obtain technical support, please contact our Customer Care Department within the United States at (866) 744-2665, or outside the United States at (510) 253-0500.

Rockridge Press publishes its books in a variety of electronic and print formats. Some content that appears in print may not be available in electronic books, and vice versa.

Photography on front cover, pages, ii, iv, v, ix, x, 13, 34, 53, 73, 109, 114, 140, and 145 © Jennifer Martiné; photography on back cover, pages vi, 10, 18, 58, 83, 116, 127, and 162 © Nadine Greeff

ISBN: Print 978-1-62315-989-4 | eBook 978-1-62315-990-0

To Cashel,
because he's the sweetest
treat of all

Contents

Introduction

When I was in fourth grade, I was assigned to write a how-to essay. It could be on any topic I wanted as long as it explained how to do something, step by step. Because I was nine years old, I loved chocolate, and I was always eager to convince my mom to let me mess up the kitchen to create the forbidden sweets I craved, I chose to write a recipe for "Dark Secret Chocolate Cake." After describing how chocolatey delicious the cake would be, my essay went on to say, "The first thing you should do is read the whole recipe and then put all the ingredients you need on the counter. If you do that, it is easy to bake a cake!" I have given this advice thousands of times since then and it still rings true. Contrary to popular belief, baking delicious, festive desserts can be simple—and even fun!

The thing about desserts is they are often made to celebrate important events such as holidays or birthdays. Because they are considered "special occasion" fare, many people think of them as being too difficult, too important, or too risky to make themselves. Of course, a birthday cake or dessert for a holiday meal *should* feel extra special, so many of us often leave the task to professional pastry chefs. But the truth is there are plenty of desserts you can make that easily fulfill the requirements of a celebratory treat, while also being simple and enjoyable enough to make yourself. These recipes are so effortless you don't even need a reason to make them.

The beauty of the Dark Secret Chocolate Cake recipe—which came from a 1969 edition of *Pillsbury's Bake Off Cake Cook Book* (don't worry, I wrote the instructions in my own words!)—was that it had only a handful of ingredients, all pantry staples, and could be made in one bowl. It was a straightforward mix-and-bake cake that even a nine-year-old could accomplish with minimal adult supervision. It was so rich and delicious it didn't require any further adornment, but when the dessert was swathed in a basic vanilla buttercream frosting it truly shone. It took little effort, but the rewards were great. That is the kind of dessert recipe you will find in this book— simple, economical, low-stress, high-reward treats suitable for even the most special of occasions, but uncomplicated enough to make any time the urge strikes.

The recipes here range from classic American treats like The Best Chocolate Chip Cookies (page 12) and Classic Gooey Chocolate Brownies (page 22) to time-saving adaptations such as No-Bake Blueberry Cheesecake Bars (page 32) and No-Bake Maple Pecan Drop Cookies (page 20); from Magic Lemon Pudding Cake (page 44) to Easy Dark Chocolate Pudding (page 41); from Butterscotch Ice Cream (page 64) to Tiramisu Ice Cream Cake (page 80); from Classic Red Velvet Cupcakes (page 102) with cream cheese frosting to Espresso Icebox Cake (page 86); from Dark Chocolate Pecan Pie (page 126) to Crustless Pear Custard Tart (page 138); and from Crispy-Crunch Honeycomb Candy (page 146) to Candy-Coated Popcorn (page 151). And the book doesn't stop at American classics, but includes favorite desserts from around the world such as Rich and Creamy Caramel Flan (page 36), Strawberry Clafoutis (page 51), Tarte Tatin (page 129), Nectarine Galette (page 133), Dark Chocolate Truffles (page 160), and Layered Mexican Coconut Candy Squares (page 150).

In addition to providing dozens of recipes, the book offers a crash course in baking and details essential techniques, basic ingredients, and both the minimal must-have equipment and those items that are nice to have but not essential. There's even a step-by-step recipe checklist to help you succeed every time.

Home cooks of any skill level can successfully master these recipes. Each includes clear, step-by-step instructions, helpful tips, and valuable technique hacks. Best of all, they use readily available and inexpensive ingredients, common everyday kitchen tools, and basic techniques. When you serve homemade desserts from this book, you're bound to have people believing you labored over them for hours or even ordered from a professional bakery. That's precisely why I call them "deceptively easy." I say, go ahead and let them think you toiled all day in the kitchen. I can keep a secret if you can.

Chapter One

EASY ESSENTIALS

TO GET STARTED

Desserts, by definition, are meant to be special. We serve them at holiday meals, birthday celebrations, weddings, and other momentous occasions and, because of that, we want each one to stand out and be indulgent. Happily, there are plenty of easy-to-make desserts that are just perfect for celebrating any number of occasions. This book is loaded with such recipes—from cookies, brownies, and bars to candies and other confections.

ESSENTIAL INGREDIENTS

As with any recipe, the end result is largely dependent on the quality of the ingredients you put in it. That doesn't mean you need exotic, rare, or hard-to-find ingredients for your dessert recipe. In fact, you will do well to stick to basic ingredients and quality brands. The following are some ingredients you'll find in this book essential to making desserts successfully.

Flour

Many baked goods—including cookies, brownies, bars, cakes, and cupcakes as well as pastry crusts—begin with flour. When we talk about flour, we generally mean wheat flour, unless otherwise specified. All-purpose flour is a type of flour with a moderate level of protein, and is typically enriched with additional nutrients and malted barley. It's called "all-purpose" because it can be used successfully for most recipes. Bread flour is ideal for making bread because it is high in protein and develops the highest levels of gluten, the substance that gives bread its chewy structure. Flours with lower protein, such as pastry flour or the even lower-protein cake flour, are ideal for recipes where you want a light, airy structure, such as cakes and pastry crusts. All-purpose flour falls in between bread flour and pastry flour on the protein spectrum and can generally be substituted for either in a pinch. Occasionally, recipes will include flours other than wheat—such as rice or almond flour. These wheat-free flours will be specified as such.

Baking Soda and Baking Powder

Baking soda and baking powder are both leaveners, but they are not interchangeable. In fact, many recipes call for both at the same time.

Baking soda, also known as a bicarbonate of soda, produces carbon dioxide when it comes into contact with acidic ingredients. This reaction causes your baked goods to rise. Acidic ingredients commonly used in baking recipes include vinegar and citrus juices, but buttermilk, brown sugar, yogurt, cream of tartar, molasses, applesauce, and honey are all acidic as well. When using baking soda in recipes, the idea is to use just enough to react with the amount of acid in the recipe and produce carbon dioxide. The acid, in turn, neutralizes the baking soda. If you use too much baking soda, you'll end up with a metallic or soapy flavor in your baked goods.

Baking powder, an ingredient made of baking soda combined with cream of tartar, is a powdered acid. The leavening reaction occurs when the powder comes in contact with wet ingredients. Baking powder is especially useful in recipes that require a leavener but that don't have acidic ingredients to activate the baking soda. Double-acting baking powder produces two leavening reactions: the first when the powder gets wet and the second when the mixture is heated. Since most baking powder you find in markets is the double-acting type, we use double-acting baking powder as our default. So when recipes in this book call for baking powder, you can assume that means double-acting baking powder.

Recipes that require both baking soda and baking powder usually contain acidic ingredients such as yogurt, brown sugar, buttermilk, or lemon juice, but not enough to provide the full leavening action needed. In these cases, baking powder is used as well to provide additional lift.

Salt

Salt is an essential ingredient in sweet recipes as it accentuates, brightens, and balances nuanced flavors, adding depth and dimension. Too much salt can make a dessert unpleasantly salty, but not enough will leave it tasting flat and unbalanced. For the recipes in this book, and for desserts in general, I recommend a fine-grained sea salt instead of either table salt (which contains unnecessary additives) or kosher salt (which is somewhat coarse and won't dissolve and disperse as quickly or evenly into your sweets).

Butter

Butter is another key ingredient in dessert recipes, particularly baked goods. Butter is the ingredient that makes cakes moist, pastries tender and flaky, and frostings creamy. In addition to being crucial to achieving the desired texture of various recipes, butter also adds flavor, so it is especially important to use good-quality butter in your recipes.

Butter is usually found in three varieties: unsalted, salted, or cultured. All three start with cream, also called sweet cream, although it does not have any added sweetener. Unsalted butter is just that, sweet cream churned into butter. Salted butter, as you might imagine, has added salt in the cream. Cultured butter is made with cultured cream, or cream that has been slightly fermented to give it a bit of a tangy flavor that provides the distinction from "sweet cream" butter. Cultured butter is more common in Europe and is usually sold unsalted. In the United States, you'll more often find European-style butter, which is unsalted, or salted butter that has had cultured cream flavor added to make it taste like the cultured butters found in Europe. Cultured or European-style butter can be substituted for sweet cream butter in most recipes, though the taste may be slightly different.

Most dessert recipes call for unsalted sweet cream butter. Using unsalted butter is important in dessert making because it allows you to control the amount of salt in the recipe. All the butter called for in this book is unsalted sweet cream butter.

Sugar

Sugar is an essential ingredient in desserts since it is what makes sweets, well, sweet. But that's not all sugar does—not by a long shot. Sugar is important for developing various textures, making treats variously tender, moist, airy, and crunchy. Because of this, using more or less sugar—or an entirely different sweetener, like honey—can affect not only just the flavor of your finished dish, but also the texture as well.

The types of sugar used in this book are all cane or beet sugars and include granulated sugar (this is what we mean when we say simply "sugar"), brown sugar (granulated sugar with molasses added), or confectioner's sugar (granulated sugar ground into a powder, often combined with a bit of cornstarch). A tip for brown sugar: to keep it soft, store it in an airtight container. Believe it or not, adding a few marshmallows to the bag also keeps it soft.

Eggs

Eggs are important in baked goods for creating structure, thickening, emulsifying, and providing leavening action, color, and flavor. The one thing you need to know about eggs while using this book is that all eggs used here are large chicken eggs. While you'll find eggs that are organic, cage-free, pastured, and have shells of white, brown, or green at your local market, none of these factors really change your results as long as you stick to large chicken eggs.

Vanilla

Vanilla adds depth and roundness to recipes. You don't necessarily notice the flavor of vanilla in a chocolate cake, but you'd notice if it was missing. Where vanilla extract is called for, use only pure vanilla extract—made by steeping vanilla beans in alcohol—rather than vanilla flavoring. Some recipes call for whole vanilla beans, which are split and scraped out or steeped in milk or cream. Vanilla paste, essentially the scooped-out insides of vanilla beans, can be substituted for vanilla beans for convenience or for vanilla extract when you don't want to use even a small amount of alcohol in your recipes.

ESSENTIAL EQUIPMENT

Every month it seems new cooking gadgets appear on the market. As tempting as it is to scoop up all these nifty doodads, it's really not necessary, at least not for making the recipes in this book. All these recipes can be made using basic equipment. In many cases, an electric handheld mixer, stand mixer, food processor, or other machinery will make the task easier and quicker, but they are not essential.

Must-Have

The following is a list of essential equipment you'll need for the recipes in this book.

BAKING SHEET A baking sheet is a flat metal sheet with a lip on one or both of the short sides for gripping. The large flat surface makes it ideal for cooking batches of cookies. The flat edges allow you to slide cookies off easily without altering their shape. They are usually made of aluminum or steel. Nonstick coatings make it easy to remove cooked items, but their darker color can accelerate browning so you may need to lower your oven temperature or reduce the cooking time.

RIMMED BAKING SHEET A rimmed baking sheet is a flat pan with a rim around the edges. It can be used for cookies, but can also be used for other things that require a rim to keep them contained. Like baking sheets, these come in aluminum, steel, and nonstick varieties.

BAKING PANS Baking pans usually have sides about 2 inches deep. They can be square (8 inches or 9 inches are most common), rectangular (8-by-11-inch or 9-by-13-inch), or round (8 inch or 9 inch). Glass and ceramic baking dishes come in the same sizes, but because they are slower than aluminum pans to both heat up and cool down, they are not ideal for baked goods such as brownies, cakes, and bars.

MEASURING CUPS & SPOONS You'll need a set of dry measuring cups and spoons designed to be filled to the rim with dry ingredients and leveled off and a standard set of measuring spoons ($\frac{1}{8}$ teaspoon, $\frac{1}{4}$ teaspoon, $\frac{1}{2}$ teaspoon, 1 teaspoon, and 1 tablespoon).

MIXING BOWLS You'll want at least 2 mixing bowls, one medium and one large. A set of metal bowls is especially handy since you can place a metal bowl over a pan of simmering water to use as a double boiler. Glass or ceramic bowls are good to have, too, and come in handy when using highly acidic ingredients that might react with metal. Plastic bowls are fine, but they should not be heated.

ELECTRIC MIXER Many recipes in this book can be made without an electric mixer, but a few are so much easier with one that I recommend using one in the instructions. This doesn't have to be a fancy stand mixer. A handheld mixer, the kind with two metal beaters, is fine.

WHISK A whisk is essential for whisking sauces, egg whites, or heavy cream into fluffy clouds, among other tasks. A good-quality whisk is inexpensive and a tool you'll appreciate having just about every time you cook. For many recipes, you can also use an electric mixer (either handheld or stand) with a whisk attachment to accomplish any required whisking.

ROLLING PIN A rolling pin is essential for making pastry crusts, biscuits, and certain types of cookies. There are two main types. The typical American-style, or baker's rolling pin, has a center rod controlled by two handles on the ends and turns inside an outer cylinder. These are usually made of wood and are easy to hold and maneuver, though on the heavy side. The French-style tapered rolling pins are just a tapered wooden rod that you push over the dough with the heels of your hands. These are lighter weight than baker's rolling pins, and give you a bit more control over the pressure you use. Either type will work for the recipes in this book, so it is really a question of personal preference.

PASTRY BRUSH A pastry, or basting, brush is useful for spreading glaze over pastries, cakes, and breads or applying an egg wash over a crust. It also comes in handy for oiling baking pans. Look for one with soft, flexible bristles that won't easily splinter or fall out. Choose from durable and easy-to-wash silicone or more delicate natural bristles.

PARCHMENT PAPER Parchment paper is similar to wax paper, but gets its nonstick property from heat-resistant silicone instead of wax, which can melt or even ignite in the oven. Like wax paper, parchment is resistant to both grease and moisture. Use it as a nonstick liner for cakes and on baking sheets, or use it to cover countertops when rolling out dough. You'll find rolls of parchment paper alongside the wax paper in most supermarkets. Baking supply and cookware stores offer precut sheets and rounds made to fit baking pans.

WIRE RACK A wire rack is essential for baking. This allows air to circulate, so all sides of your cookies, cakes, or cupcakes cool at the same rate. Not only do baked goods cool faster on a rack, but also removing them from the hot pan and putting them on the rack quickly stops them from cooking further or overbaking. The full air circulation also serves to prevent hot steam from turning into condensation and making your baked goods soggy.

Nice-to-Have

Cookware stores are full of useful-looking gadgets. Their promises of making cooking easier or more fun are tempting. If you already own the essentials listed previously and want to add more tools to your kitchen arsenal, the following items are certainly nice to have.

COOKIE SCOOPS Cookie scoops, which come in several sizes from small to large, are inexpensive and useful to have around if you make lots of cookies. They'll save you a lot of time versus having to form each cookie by hand. They can also be used for making meatballs and other kitchen tasks.

SILICONE BAKING MATS Mats made of flexible, heat-resistant silicone are pricier than parchment paper, but can be used over and over to provide a nonstick surface on which to cook your baked goods.

STAND MIXER Stand mixers are pricey, but if you do a lot of baking they are worth the money considering how much effort they save. The great thing about a stand mixer is that you can have it running and still have your hands free for adding ingredients. When making things such as buttercream frosting, which needs to be whipped for several minutes at a time, this appliance lets you attend to other things while you wait for the mixture to thicken.

SCALE Some recipes, particularly baking recipes or recipes from European cooks, give dry goods measurements by weight rather than volume. A digital scale that measures in ounces/pounds and grams/kilos is useful, but all recipes in this book use volume measurements.

ESSENTIAL CHECKLIST

Here is a handy step-by-step checklist you can apply to any recipe when making desserts to help ensure your endeavors are successful.

- **Read the recipe in its entirety before starting.** This key step should always be the first thing you do—before you begin preparing the recipe. You don't want to get halfway through preparations for a dessert to be served later that evening only to discover a step that calls for refrigerating the ingredients overnight.

- **Preheat the oven.** Preheating the oven before baking is essential. You want to bake your foods at the proper temperature from the beginning. This is important for controlling cooking time and making sure the dish cooks the way the recipe intends.

- **Use the appropriate measuring cups for liquid and dry ingredients.** Dry measuring cups are designed to be filled to the rim with dry ingredients and leveled off with a knife or other flat-edged object. Liquid measuring cups are transparent, have incremental measurement markings on the side, and a pouring spout. Using the right type of measuring cup for your ingredients is crucial to obtain accurate measurements.

- **Let your ingredients come to room temperature before starting the recipe.** When a recipe calls for ingredients, such as butter or eggs, to be at room temperature, there's a good reason. Combined at room temperature, these ingredients form an emulsion that traps air. That air expands as it is heated, resulting in fluffy, airy, and light baked goods. If the ingredients are cold when you start, they won't be able to trap as much air and will result in flatter, denser baked goods. Using room temperature ingredients also helps create a smoother, more evenly textured batter.

- **Temper ingredients when mixing hot with cold.** If you plop room temperature eggs into a pot of hot cream, you'll end up with lumpy scrambled eggs in cream. Instead, slowly stir a small amount of hot cream into the eggs to bring their temperature up. When you mix the two, the temperature change will be gradual enough that it won't instantly cook the eggs.

- **Do not overwork the dough once flour has been added.** When you beat flour into cake batter or cookie dough, the flour begins to develop gluten. Gluten is what gives bread that nice chewiness— but you don't want that in your cookies and cakes. To avoid overworking the dough, once you've added the flour to your mix, continue mixing or beating just until the flour is fully incorporated.

Grease the baking sheet or pan, or use parchment paper to line it. Follow instructions for greasing and lining baking sheets or pans. When a recipe calls for greasing or lining a pan, know that if you skip this step, your dish will likely stick to the pan. If the recipe instructs you to put the batter or dough in an ungreased or unlined pan, it means the recipe has enough fat in it that the dish will not stick, so go ahead, leave it bare.

Bake on the oven's middle rack. The oven's middle rack is usually where you'll find the most even heat, so most recipes should be cooked on the middle rack unless otherwise instructed. Also, ovens vary, so if yours gets hotter at the top than the bottom or vice versa, keep that in mind when deciding where to situate the rack.

Check for doneness at the minimum time. Since ovens vary, it's difficult for a recipe to indicate exactly how long a dish needs to cook. When a range is given (such as 18 to 22 minutes), always check for doneness at the minimum time (18 minutes). This helps avoid overcooking.

Let baked goods cool properly. I know, I know. It's *so hard* to wait for sweet, buttery, delicious-smelling treats to cool before you indulge. But you have to. No, really. It's important. Baked goods retain heat and steam even after they come out of the oven, and this heat and steam complete the baking process. If you let it out early, your baked goods may end up doughy or gummy in the center. Furthermore, if you release all that steam before the process is finished, your baked goods will lose moisture, making them dry.

Chapter 2

COOKIES, BROWNIES & BARS

Left: Classic Gooey Chocolate Brownies (page 22)

THE BEST
CHOCOLATE CHIP COOKIES

⊷ Makes about 24 cookies ⊶

It's fitting that the first recipe in this book is one for chocolate chip cookies, since it very well may be the most common first recipe anyone makes. I remember making chocolate chip cookies with my mom, with babysitters, and then, when I was a little older, with my friends. They're a breeze to make, always satisfying, and use ingredients probably in your kitchen at this very moment! The secret ingredient is the melted butter, which makes the cookies unbelievably soft and chewy.

PREP TIME: **10 minutes**

BAKE TIME: **9 to 11 minutes**

EQUIPMENT: **Baking sheet**

½ cup (1 stick) unsalted butter, melted
½ cup granulated sugar
¼ cup packed light brown sugar
1 teaspoon vanilla extract
1 egg
1½ cups all-purpose flour
¾ teaspoon salt
½ teaspoon baking soda
¾ cup semisweet chocolate chips

1. Preheat the oven to 350°F.

2. In a large bowl, with a wooden spoon, electric mixer, or in the bowl of a stand mixer, cream together the butter, granulated sugar, and brown sugar until creamy.

3. Add the vanilla and egg. Mix just until incorporated.

4. Add the flour, salt, and baking soda. Mix until the mixture clumps.

5. Mix in the chocolate chips. Drop the batter by rounded tablespoons onto an ungreased baking sheet, leaving about 2 inches in between each cookie. Bake for 9 to 11 minutes until the cookies are pale golden brown.

6. Remove from the oven and let the cookies cool on the sheet for about 30 seconds. Transfer to a wire rack and let cool completely. Store at room temperature in an airtight container for several days.

Ingredient tip: Use chocolate chunks in place of chocolate chips, or use equal parts chunks and chips. You can also add ¾ cup chopped nuts, such as walnuts, pecans, or hazelnuts, if you like.

ICED BROWN BUTTER OATMEAL COOKIES

⟫ Makes about 18 cookies ⟪

Oatmeal cookies are like a warm hug from your favorite friend—comforting, familiar, and full of love. Believe it or not, these are even better than the ones you're probably accustomed to. Browning the butter before mixing it in the cookie dough adds deep, round, nutty, caramel-y flavor notes. The sweet glaze makes them even more special.

PREP TIME: **10 minutes**
BAKE TIME: **10 to 12 minutes**
EQUIPMENT: **Medium skillet, baking sheet**

FOR THE COOKIES
1 cup (2 sticks) unsalted butter
1 cup packed light brown sugar
½ cup granulated sugar
2 teaspoons vanilla extract
2 eggs, at room temperature
2 cups all-purpose flour
2 cups old-fashioned rolled oats
1 teaspoon baking soda
1 teaspoon ground cinnamon
¼ teaspoon salt

FOR THE ICING
1 cup powdered sugar
1 teaspoon vanilla extract
2 tablespoons low-fat or whole milk

TO MAKE THE COOKIES

1. Preheat the oven to 350°F.

2. In a medium skillet set over medium heat, melt the butter and let it cook until it begins to foam, begins to brown, and smells toasty and nutty. Immediately remove the skillet from the heat and scrape the butter into a large bowl.

3. Add the brown sugar and granulated sugar. Using an electric mixer or wooden spoon, mix until well combined.

4. Add the vanilla and eggs, and beat until smooth.

5. Add the flour, oats, baking soda, cinnamon, and salt and beat until just combined. Drop the dough onto a baking sheet in heaping tablespoons, leaving about 2 inches between cookies. Bake for 10 to 12 minutes, until the cookies are golden brown around the edges.

6. Remove from the oven and let cool on the baking sheet for 2 to 3 minutes before transferring the cookies to a wire rack to cool completely. Store in an airtight container for up to 2 weeks.

TO MAKE THE ICING

In a medium bowl, stir together the powdered sugar, vanilla, and milk until smooth. Once the cookies have cooled for a few minutes, spoon the icing onto them, using about 2 teaspoons per cookie.

Ingredient tip: You can substitute whole-wheat flour for the all-purpose flour. This will add another layer of flavor and also make the cookies a wee bit healthier.

CHEWY
GINGER COOKIES

⟺ Makes about 24 cookies ⟺

With a perfect balance of spices, a crackly sugarcoated exterior,
and a lovely chewy texture, these ginger cookies are pure goodness.
Eat them warm just out of the oven or at room temperature any time
of day with a hot cup of coffee or tea or a tall glass of cold milk.

PREP TIME: **10 minutes**
BAKE TIME: **12 to 15 minutes**
EQUIPMENT: **2 baking sheets,
medium bowl, large bowl**

1½ cups sugar, divided
2¼ cups all-purpose flour
2 teaspoons ground ginger
1 teaspoon ground cinnamon
1 teaspoon baking soda
½ teaspoon ground cloves
½ teaspoon salt
½ cup (1 stick) unsalted butter,
    at room temperature
⅓ cup molasses
1 egg

1. Preheat the oven to 375°F.

2. Line 2 baking sheets with parchment paper, and put ½ cup of the sugar in a shallow bowl.

3. In a medium bowl, whisk the flour, ginger, cinnamon, baking soda, cloves, and salt.

4. In a large bowl, with a wooden spoon or electric mixer, cream together the butter and the remaining 1 cup of sugar.

5. Add the molasses and egg and continue to beat until the dough lightens. Add the dry ingredients and mix until thoroughly incorporated. With your hands, form the dough into 1-inch balls. Roll each ball in the bowl of sugar to coat lightly. Arrange the dough balls 2 inches apart on the prepared sheets. Bake for 12 to 15 minutes until the cookies are cracked and golden brown.

6. Remove from the oven and let the cookies cool on the baking sheet for 5 minutes before transferring them to a wire rack to cool completely. Store in an airtight container for up to 2 weeks.

Technique tip: For best results, bake these cookies in 3 batches. While the first batch is in the oven, form and coat the second batch. Follow the same pattern for the third batch.

NO-BAKE
WHITE CHOCOLATE
CRISP COOKIES

⫸ Makes about 50 cookies ⫷

These are like a grown-up version of Rice Krispies Treats, but happily still totally kid friendly. What I love most about these cookies is the rich flavor of white chocolate. But my second favorite thing is that they can be made in minutes without even turning on the oven. And, did I mention the fact that they only contain four ingredients?

PREP TIME: **10 minutes**
CHILLING TIME: **30 minutes**
EQUIPMENT: **2 baking sheets,** microwave or double boiler

2 cups crisped rice cereal
1 cup mini marshmallows
½ cup creamy peanut butter
1 pound chopped white chocolate,
    or white chocolate chips

1. Line 2 baking sheets with parchment paper.

2. In a large bowl, stir together the cereal and marshmallows.

3. In a large microwave-safe bowl, combine the peanut butter and white chocolate. Microwave at 50 percent power, in 30-second intervals, stirring in between, until completely melted and smooth. Pour the mixture over the cereal and marshmallows and stir to coat completely.

4. Using a tablespoon, drop the mixture on the prepared sheets. Refrigerate until the chocolate sets, about 30 minutes. Serve immediately or refrigerate in an airtight container, separated by sheets of parchment, for up to 1 week.

Ingredient tip: These pale, lumpy cookies beg to be decorated. After dropping the dough onto the baking sheets, before it begins to harden, sprinkle the cookies with ¼ cup mini chocolate chips, colorful sprinkles, shredded coconut, chopped nuts, or any other delightful decoration that strikes your fancy.

GOOEY CHOCOLATE BROWNIES

Makes 16 brownies

There is no occasion—even the happiest kind—that can't be drastically improved by a good, classic, chocolatey brownie. Made with unsweetened chocolate, these brownies pack deep cocoa-rich flavor. With just enough flour to hold them together, they are gooey and utterly perfect. The fact that they can be stirred together in a single bowl in just a few minutes makes this recipe a definite keeper.

PREP TIME: **5 minutes**

COOK TIME: **30 to 35 minutes**

EQUIPMENT: **8-inch square baking pan**

½ cup (1 stick) unsalted butter, plus
   more for preparing the pan,
   at room temperature

2 ounces unsweetened chocolate,
   finely chopped

2 eggs, at room temperature

1 teaspoon vanilla extract

1 cup sugar

¼ cup all-purpose flour

¼ teaspoon salt

1. Preheat the oven to 325°F.

2. Generously grease an 8-inch square baking pan with butter.

3. Either in a saucepan set over medium heat or in a microwave-safe bowl, combine the butter and chocolate. Heat, or microwave at 50 percent power, in 30-second intervals, until both are completely melted and the mixture is smooth. Remove from the heat and set aside to cool for several minutes.

4. In a large bowl, whisk the butter-chocolate mixture with the eggs and vanilla until incorporated.

5. Add the sugar, flour, and salt and stir to mix well. Transfer the batter to the prepared pan and bake for 30 to 35 minutes.

6. Remove from the oven and let cool before cutting the brownies into bars. Serve immediately or store in an airtight container at room temperature for up to 5 days.

Ingredient tip: If you like nuts in your brownies, add 1 cup toasted walnuts, almonds, hazelnuts, or pecans along with the sugar, flour, and salt.

CHOCOLATE BROWNIES

— Makes 16 brownies —

When you desperately need a pan of brownies but don't have the time to bake, this recipe is your answer. Three ingredients are stirred together, spread in a brownie pan, and refrigerated until set. What could be easier? The best thing is that these brownies are *so* good.

PREP TIME: 10 minutes

CHILLING TIME: 3 hours

EQUIPMENT: 9-inch square baking pan

Nonstick baking spray
1 (14-ounce) can sweetened
    condensed milk
2 ounces unsweetened chocolate,
    finely chopped
2 ½ cups graham cracker crumbs

1. Spray a 9-inch square baking pan with baking spray.

2. In a medium saucepan set over medium-low heat, combine the sweetened condensed milk and chocolate. Cook for about 10 minutes, stirring constantly, until the chocolate is completely melted and the mixture is smooth. Remove the pan from the heat.

3. Add the graham cracker crumbs to the saucepan and stir to mix well. Transfer the mixture to the prepared baking pan and spread it into an even layer. Place the pan in the refrigerator and chill for at least 3 hours until well set. Slice into bars and serve chilled or refrigerate, covered, for up to 1 week.

Technique tip: Turn graham crackers into crumbs by pulsing them in a food processor or blender, or put them in a large resealable plastic bag and crush them with a rolling pin or any heavy, cylindrical object (like a wine bottle or an unopened can of tomatoes).

SALTED CARAMEL-STUFFED FUDGE BROWNIES

— Makes about 24 brownies —

There are times when a regular old brownie just won't do. Times like those call for a spectacular, oozing, salty-sweet, fudge-and-caramel-filled extravaganza of a brownie. Look no farther—this is that brownie. Some might call it over the top, but I call it perfection.

PREP TIME: **10 minutes**
COOK TIME: **47 to 52 minutes**
EQUIPMENT: **9-by-13-inch baking pan**

Nonstick baking spray
1½ cups all-purpose flour
1 teaspoon salt
1 teaspoon baking powder
2 cups sugar
¾ cup unsweetened cocoa powder
1 cup neutral-flavored oil (such
   as grapeseed, safflower, or
   sunflower seed)
4 eggs
¼ cup low-fat or whole milk
1 cup (6 ounces) semisweet
   chocolate chips
1 (11-ounce) package caramels or
   caramel pieces (such as Kraft Vanilla
   Caramels or Kraft Caramel Bits)
1 (14-ounce) can sweetened
   condensed milk
1 teaspoon coarse sea salt

1. Preheat the oven to 350°F.

2. Line a 9-by-13-inch baking pan with parchment paper, and spray the parchment with baking spray.

3. In a medium bowl, stir together the flour, salt, and baking powder.

4. In a large bowl, with a wooden spoon or electric mixer, mix the sugar, cocoa powder, oil, eggs, and milk until well combined and smooth.

5. Add the flour mixture and stir or beat until incorporated.

6. Stir in the chocolate chips. Spoon ⅔ of the batter into the prepared pan and bake for 12 minutes.

7. Meanwhile, in a medium microwave-safe bowl, combine the caramels and sweetened condensed milk. Microwave at 50 percent power, in 30-second intervals, until the caramel melts and the mixture is smooth.

8. Remove the partially baked brownies from the oven and pour the melted caramel mixture over the top, spreading it into an even layer. Sprinkle the coarse sea salt over the caramel and then drop the remaining brownie batter on top in heaping spoonfuls. Using a butter knife, gently swirl together the caramel and brownie mixtures. Return to the oven and bake for 35 to 40 minutes more, until set and a toothpick inserted into the center comes out clean.

9. Remove from the oven and let the brownies cool completely before slicing and serving. Store in an airtight container at room temperature for up to 1 week.

Ingredient tip: Choose a good quality coarse sea salt for this recipe, such as sel gris or fleur de sel. The flaky texture of the pyramid-shaped sea salt grains adds a pleasing crunch and the coarser varieties won't dissolve after sprinkling.

BROWN SUGAR AND BUTTERSCOTCH BLONDIES

—— Makes about 16 blondies ——

I know there are people—lots of them—who think a dessert isn't really a dessert if it doesn't have chocolate in it. Thanks to desserts like this one, I will never be one of those people. I won't argue that chocolate isn't amazing, but the rich, round caramel notes of dark brown sugar, melted butter, and vanilla are intensely inviting in their own rights. Baking them together into a dense, gooey bar with the texture of a chocolate brownie lets these flavors shine.

PREP TIME: **5 minutes**

COOK TIME: **25 to 30 minutes**

EQUIPMENT: **8-inch square baking pan**

½ cup (1 stick) unsalted butter, melted, plus more for preparing the baking pan
1 cup packed dark brown sugar
1 egg, lightly beaten
1 teaspoon vanilla extract
1 cup all-purpose flour
½ teaspoon baking powder
⅛ teaspoon baking soda
Pinch salt
⅓ cup butterscotch chips

1. Preheat the oven to 350°F.

2. Generously grease an 8-inch square baking pan with butter.

3. In a large bowl, whisk the melted butter with the brown sugar.

4. Whisk in the egg and vanilla.

5. Add the flour, baking powder, baking soda, and salt, and mix to combine.

6. Stir in the butterscotch chips. Transfer the batter to the prepared pan and spread into an even layer. Bake for 25 to 30 minutes, until a toothpick inserted into the center comes out clean.

7. Remove from the oven and let the blondies cool before cutting into bars and serving. Store in an airtight container at room temperature for up to 1 week.

Variation tip: Add a little crunch to these blondies by adding 1 cup chopped, toasted nuts—such as walnuts, hazelnuts, or pecans—when you add the butterscotch chips.

NO-BAKE
TANGY LEMON BARS

⚛— Makes about 30 bars —⚛

These lemon bars require only seven ingredients, but are surprisingly tangy and rich. You'll love the rave reviews they get from anyone who tries them. In the summertime, their tartness is refreshing. In winter, they'll cheer up even the gloomiest day. In other words, you can't go wrong with these any time of year.

PREP TIME: **10 minutes**
CHILLING TIME: **Overnight**
EQUIPMENT: **9-by-13-inch baking pan**

10 graham crackers, crushed
2 teaspoons lemon zest
Juice of 2 ½ lemons
1 (14-ounce) can sweetened condensed milk
1 ½ cups powdered sugar, plus more for dusting
3 tablespoons unsalted butter, melted
3 tablespoons low-fat or whole milk

1. Line the bottom of a 9-by-13-inch baking pan with the crushed graham crackers.

2. In a medium bowl, whisk the lemon zest, lemon juice, and sweetened condensed milk until well combined. Pour the mixture evenly over the graham crackers.

3. In another medium bowl, stir together the powdered sugar, butter, and milk until well combined. Pour that mixture over the lemon juice mixture in the pan. Cover the pan and refrigerate overnight.

4. To serve, dust the top generously with powdered sugar, cut into 2-inch squares, and serve. Cover any leftovers with plastic wrap and keep refrigerated for up to 3 days.

Substitution tip: These bars are just as tangy-delicious made with lime juice and zest instead of lemon, especially if you can find key limes.

PB & J BARS

A delightful dessert version of everyone's favorite sandwich from childhood, these bars are a hit with young and old alike. Use any type of fruit jam or preserves you prefer. My favorite is strawberry, but blackberry, raspberry, blueberry, or grape all are tasty options. Serve these bars like you would a peanut butter and jelly sandwich—with a tall glass of cold milk.

PREP TIME: **10 minutes**
COOK TIME: **35 minutes**
EQUIPMENT: **9-by-13-inch baking pan**

1 cup (2 sticks) unsalted butter, melted, plus more for preparing the baking pan
2¼ cups all-purpose flour
½ teaspoon salt
½ teaspoon baking soda
¼ teaspoon baking powder
1 cup packed dark brown sugar
½ cup granulated sugar
1½ cups crunchy peanut butter
2 eggs, lightly beaten
2 teaspoons vanilla extract
1 cup fruit jam or preserves of choice

1. Preheat the oven to 350°F.

2. Generously grease a 9-by-13-inch baking pan with butter.

3. In a medium bowl, whisk the flour, salt, baking soda, and baking powder.

4. In a large bowl, with a wooden spoon or rubber spatula, stir together the brown sugar, granulated sugar, and melted butter, mashing the sugar into the butter as you stir, until the mixture is smooth and creamy.

5. Add the peanut butter and stir until the mixture is smooth and well combined.

6. Stir in the eggs and vanilla until incorporated.

7. Add the flour mixture and stir until combined. Transfer the batter to the prepared pan.

8. Using the back of a spoon, make little wells, evenly spaced, all over the top of the batter. Fill each well with a spoonful of jam or preserves. With a knife, swirl the jam through the batter. Bake for about 35 minutes, until a toothpick inserted in the center comes out clean.

9. Remove from the oven and set the pan on a wire rack to cool completely for about 1 hour.

10. Cut into 2-inch squares and serve immediately or wrap in plastic wrap and store at room temperature for up to 5 days.

Technique tip: To make these bars easy to slice and serve, place a long piece of foil into the pan, long enough to hang over the sides before filling the pan with the batter. After baking and cooling, place a cutting board on top of the baking pan and invert it. Lift off the pan and peel the foil off the bars. Use a second cutting board to invert the bars again so they are right-side up.

COOKIES 'N' CREAM BARS

— Makes about 30 bars —

What do you get when you combine dark chocolate, white chocolate, cream cheese, and cream-filled chocolate sandwich cookies? An irresistible treat. Because the recipe starts with store-bought cookies, it's surprisingly easy to put together! If you love the combination of sweet creamy filling and crunchy chocolate wafers, this is the dessert for you.

PREP TIME: **10 minutes**

CHILLING TIME: **2 hours**

EQUIPMENT: **9-inch square baking pan**

FOR THE CRUST
24 cream-filled chocolate sandwich
   cookies, finely crushed
¼ cup (½ stick) unsalted butter, melted

FOR THE FILLING
¾ cup white chocolate chips
6 ounces cream cheese,
   at room temperature
12 cream-filled chocolate sandwich
   cookies, coarsely chopped

FOR THE TOPPING
6 cream-filled chocolate sandwich
   cookies, coarsely chopped
¾ cup semisweet chocolate chips

TO MAKE THE CRUST

1. Line a 9-inch square baking pan with parchment paper.

2. In a medium bowl, stir together the cookie crumbs and butter until well combined. Press the mixture into the bottom of the prepared pan.

TO MAKE THE FILLING

1. In a medium microwave-safe bowl, microwave the white chocolate at 50 percent power, in 30-second intervals, stirring in between, until completely melted and smooth.

2. Add the cream cheese and stir until smooth.

3. Add the chopped cookies and stir to mix. Spread the filling evenly over the crust.

1. Sprinkle the chopped cookies evenly over the filling.

2. In a small microwave-safe bowl, microwave the chocolate chips at 50 percent power, at 30-second intervals, stirring in between, until melted and smooth. Drizzle the melted chocolate over the top. Cover and refrigerate for at least 2 hours until firm and set.

3. Slice into 2-inch squares and serve. Cover any remaining bars with plastic wrap and keep refrigerated for up to 3 days.

Technique tip: To make the cookie crumbs, pulse the cookies in a food processor or blender, or put them in a large resealable plastic bag and crush them with a rolling pin or any heavy, cylindrical object (like a wine bottle or an unopened can of tomatoes).

NO-BAKE
BLUEBERRY CHEESECAKE BARS

⸘— Makes about 16 bars —⸘

With a creamy cheesecake filling, a crunchy graham cracker crust, and
a sweet blueberry topping, these bars are like little squares of heaven.
They're an obvious go-to during blueberry season when you find
yourself with an abundance of fresh berries, but they are every bit as
good made with frozen berries so you can enjoy them any time of year.

PREP TIME: **15 minutes**
CHILLING TIME: **2 hours**
EQUIPMENT: **8-inch square baking pan**

FOR THE CRUST
10 graham crackers, crushed
　　(about 2 cups)
¼ cup sugar
½ cup (1 stick) unsalted butter, melted

FOR THE FILLING
2 (8-ounce) packages cream cheese,
　　at room temperature
1 cup powdered sugar
2 cups heavy (whipping) cream
1 teaspoon vanilla extract

FOR THE SAUCE
2 cups fresh or frozen blueberries
½ cup sugar
1 tablespoon unsalted butter
2 teaspoons cornstarch
1 teaspoon vanilla extract

TO MAKE THE CRUST

In a medium bowl, stir together the crushed
graham crackers, sugar, and butter until well
combined. Press the mixture into an 8-inch
square baking pan in an even layer.

TO MAKE THE FILLING

1. In a large bowl, using either a stand mixer
with a whisk attachment or a handheld
mixer or whisk, whisk the cream cheese
and powdered sugar until smooth.

2. Whisk in the cream and vanilla and
continue whisking for several minutes until
the mixture thickens. Pour the filling over
the crust. Cover and refrigerate for at least
2 hours, until firm.

TO MAKE THE SAUCE

1. In a medium saucepan set over medium-high heat, combine the blueberries, sugar, butter, cornstarch, and vanilla. Cover and cook for about 5 minutes until the blueberries break down and the sauce thickens. Remove from the heat and let cool. Refrigerate until ready to serve.

2. To serve, pour the blueberry sauce over the chilled cheesecake, cut into squares, and serve. Cover any leftovers with plastic wrap and keep refrigerated for up to 3 days.

Substitution tip: Substitute strawberries, blackberries, cherries, peaches, or other fruits for the blueberries. The results are sure to please.

Chapter 3

CUSTARD, PUDDING & GELATIN

Left: Classic Chocolate Mousse (page 54)

RICH AND CREAMY
CARAMEL FLAN

⟡— Serves 4 —⟡

Call it flan or crème caramel or flipped caramel
custard, it's all creamy, dreamy, delicious.

PREP TIME: **20 minutes**

COOK TIME: **45 minutes**

CHILLING TIME: **3 hours**

EQUIPMENT: **4 (6-ounce) ramekins,**
a deep baking dish large enough
to hold the ramekins, 2 saucepans,
fine-mesh sieve

FOR THE CARAMEL

Unsalted butter, for preparing
   the ramekins

½ cup sugar

5 tablespoons boiling water

FOR THE CUSTARD

4 egg yolks

2 eggs

¼ cup sugar, divided

1½ cups low-fat or whole milk

1 teaspoon vanilla extract

TO MAKE THE CARAMEL

1. Preheat the oven to 275°F.

2. Lightly grease the ramekins with butter.

3. In a small saucepan over medium heat, heat the sugar for about 5 minutes, tilting and swirling the pan until it is completely melted and lightly browned.

4. Carefully add the boiling water. Swirl the pan until the water and caramel are well combined. Remove from the heat.

5. Divide the caramel mixture evenly among the prepared ramekins, tilting the ramekins to ensure that the caramel evenly coats the entire bottom of each. Place the ramekins into the baking dish and fill the dish with enough water to come about 2 inches up the sides of the ramekins.

TO MAKE THE CUSTARD

1. In a medium bowl, whisk the egg yolks, eggs, and 2½ tablespoons of sugar.

2. In a clean saucepan set over medium-low heat, combine the milk and the remaining 1½ tablespoons of sugar. When the milk just begins to boil, pour it into a spouted measuring cup.

3. While whisking the eggs constantly, add the milk in a slow, steady stream until the mixture is well combined. Strain the mixture through a fine-mesh sieve into a bowl.

4. Pour or ladle the mixture into the ramekins, dividing evenly. Cover the baking pan with aluminum foil and carefully transfer it to the oven. Bake for 45 minutes.

5. Remove the pan from the oven, but leave the foil cover on until the custards cool completely.

6. Transfer the foil-covered baking dish to the refrigerator and chill the custards for at least 3 hours.

7. To serve, run a thin-bladed knife around the inside of each ramekin to loosen the custard. Place a serving plate over one of the ramekins and carefully invert it to unmold the custard. If the custard fails to release from the ramekin, leave the ramekin upside down on the plate. As the custard warms and gravity asserts itself, the custard should release. Serve immediately. Cover any leftovers with plastic wrap and refrigerate for up to 3 days.

Technique tip: It's important to temper the yolk mixture by adding a small amount of hot liquid and whisking vigorously to bring the temperature of the yolks up to that of the milk mixture. If you don't, the eggs will scramble and you'll end up with lumpy custard.

CINNAMON CUSTARD

— Serves 4 —

This delightfully spiced custard is a snap to make, but the
flavor is so rich and unexpected it is a guaranteed showstopper.
The best part is that it is made from ingredients you may have
in your kitchen right now. What are you waiting for?

PREP TIME: **5 minutes**
COOK TIME: **10 minutes**
EQUIPMENT: **Medium saucepan,
fine-mesh sieve**

½ cup sugar
2 (3-inch) cinnamon sticks, broken
1 cup low-fat or whole milk
1 cup heavy (whipping) cream
6 egg yolks, at room temperature
1 tablespoon cornstarch
Ground cinnamon, for garnish

1. Spread the sugar over the bottom of a
medium saucepan set over medium heat.
Add the cinnamon sticks and cook for about
5 minutes just until the sugar melts and
turns golden.

2. Carefully pour in the milk and cream,
being careful not to splatter, and bring
the mixture to a boil.

3. In a large bowl, whisk the egg yolks and
cornstarch. While whisking continuously,
slowly add the hot milk mixture to the yolks.
Return the mixture to the saucepan and
place it over medium heat. Cook for about
5 minutes, stirring, until it thickens.

4. Strain the thickened mixture through
a fine-mesh sieve into a serving bowl, discarding the cinnamon sticks. Garnish with
a bit of ground cinnamon and serve warm.
Cover any leftovers with plastic wrap and
refrigerate for up to 3 days.

Technique tip: As with the Rich and Creamy
Caramel Flan (see tip page 37), it is important
to add the hot milk mixture to the egg mixture
slowly, whisking continuously, so you don't
scramble the eggs.

BAKED
PLUM CUSTARD

— Serves 6 —

Nothing says summer like fresh, ripe stone fruit. This dessert makes the most of that summer bounty. The recipe calls for plums, but you can substitute any stone fruit, such as peaches, nectarines, or cherries. The sweet fruit caramelizes in the oven's heat as it nestles into the creamy, rich custard.

PREP TIME: 10 minutes
COOK TIME: 45 minutes to 1 hour
EQUIPMENT: 9-inch pie dish, fine-mesh sieve

Unsalted butter, for preparing the pan
1¼ cups low-fat or whole milk
⅓ cup sugar
2 eggs
½ cup all-purpose flour
1 tablespoon vanilla extract
⅛ teaspoon salt
4 plums, pitted and quartered
Powdered sugar, for garnish

1. Preheat the oven to 350°F.

2. Generously grease a 9-inch pie dish with butter.

3. In a medium bowl, whisk the milk, sugar, eggs, flour, vanilla, and salt. Strain the mixture through a fine-mesh sieve into the prepared pie dish.

4. Arrange the plum wedges on top of the batter.

5. Bake for 45 minutes to 1 hour until the cake is puffed, golden brown, and a toothpick inserted into the center comes out clean.

6. Garnish with powdered sugar, slice, and serve warm or at room temperature. Cover any leftovers with plastic wrap and refrigerate for up to 3 days.

Technique tip: Don't skip the step of straining the mixture through a fine-mesh sieve. This is key to making a silky-smooth custard.

ARBORIO RICE PUDDING

Rice pudding is a soothing dessert and the perfect thing on a cold evening. This version starts with uncooked rice, so it couldn't be any easier to make. Add a cup of raisins along with the butter and vanilla, if you like.

PREP TIME: **15 minutes (including 10 minutes to soak the rice)**

COOK TIME: **1 hour**

EQUIPMENT: **Medium saucepan, 8-inch square baking dish**

2 tablespoons unsalted butter, plus more for preparing the baking dish
1 cup uncooked arborio rice
2 cups whole milk
½ cup heavy (whipping) cream
Pinch salt
¼ cup sugar
1 teaspoon vanilla extract
½ teaspoon ground cinnamon

1. Preheat the oven to 325°F.

2. Generously grease an 8-inch square baking dish with butter.

3. In a medium saucepan, combine the rice, milk, cream, and salt. Let the rice soak for 10 minutes.

4. Place the saucepan over medium-high heat and bring just to a boil. Remove the saucepan from the heat and pour the rice mixture into the prepared dish.

5. Stir in the butter, sugar, and vanilla.

6. Sprinkle the cinnamon over the top. Bake for about 1 hour, until the rice is tender, all the liquid has been soaked up, and the top is golden brown.

7. Remove from the oven and serve warm. Cover any leftovers with plastic wrap and refrigerate for up to 3 days.

Ingredient tip: Arborio rice is a short-grained white rice from Italy. It is the rice commonly used to make risotto as it cooks to a delightfully creamy texture, making it the perfect choice for rice pudding. If you can't find arborio rice, substitute any short-grained white rice.

DARK CHOCOLATE PUDDING

⊰⊱ Serves 4 ⊰⊱

Homemade, from scratch, chocolate pudding is both an indulgent comfort food and an elegant dessert. This one gets deep chocolate flavor from both cocoa powder and dark chocolate. Serve it warm or chilled, topped with a dollop of sweetened whipped cream and a dusting of chocolate shavings to make it extra fancy for company.

PREP TIME: **5 minutes**

COOK TIME: **4 minutes**

EQUIPMENT: **Medium saucepan**

¼ cup cornstarch

3 tablespoons unsweetened cocoa powder

⅓ cup sugar

¼ teaspoon salt

3 cups whole milk

4 ounces dark chocolate, melted in the microwave (see tip)

2 teaspoons vanilla extract

1. In a large saucepan, whisk the cornstarch, cocoa powder, sugar, and salt.

2. Add the milk and whisk until well combined. Place the saucepan over medium heat and bring to a simmer. Cook for about 4 minutes, whisking continuously, until the mixture thickens. Transfer the hot mixture to a medium bowl.

3. Whisk in the melted chocolate and vanilla. Serve immediately or cover with plastic wrap and refrigerate for up to 3 days.

Ingredient tip: For best results, use a good-quality dark chocolate that contains 70 percent or higher cocoa solids. To melt the chocolate, chop it, put it in a microwave-safe dish, and microwave at 50 percent power, in 30-second intervals, stirring in between, until thoroughly melted and smooth.

CREAMY
MANGO PUDDING

— Serves 8 —

This simple pudding is thickened with gelatin, making it pretty much foolproof. The result is a pretty, yellow, silky-smooth pudding bursting with the tropical flavor of mango. This is a refreshing dessert to serve after a spicy meal and goes particularly well with Chinese food.

PREP TIME: **5 minutes**

COOK TIME: **10 minutes**

CHILLING TIME: **2 hours**

EQUIPMENT: **8 (6-ounce) ramekins, small saucepan, blender or food processor, fine-mesh sieve**

1¼ cups sugar, divided
2½ cups cold water, divided
1 pound frozen mango chunks
2 (¼-ounce) packets unflavored gelatin
½ teaspoon salt
1 cup heavy (whipping) cream, chilled
1 teaspoon freshly squeezed lime juice

1. Arrange 8 (6-ounce) ramekins on a baking sheet.

2. In a small saucepan set over medium-high heat, combine ½ cup of sugar with ¾ cup of cold water and heat for about 4 minutes, stirring, until the sugar fully dissolves and the mixture comes to a boil.

3. In a blender or food processor, combine the frozen mango and sugar mixture. Process until smooth. Strain the mixture through a fine-mesh sieve into a medium bowl, discarding any solids.

4. In a small saucepan set over high heat, bring 1¼ cups water to a boil.

5. In a large bowl, whisk the remaining ¾ cup of sugar with the gelatin and salt.

6. Whisk in the remaining ½ cup of cold water and continue to whisk for about 30 seconds. Add the boiling water and continue to whisk for about 1 minute until the sugar and gelatin completely dissolve.

7. Stir in 2 cups of mango purée along with the heavy cream and lime juice, mixing until well combined. Spoon the mixture into the ramekins, dividing evenly. Refrigerate for at least 2 hours until firm. Serve chilled. Cover any leftovers with plastic wrap and refrigerate for up to 3 days.

Substitution tip : To make this dairy free, substitute an equal amount of canned coconut milk for the heavy cream. The result will be just as thick and creamy, but with the added flavor of coconut, which pairs wonderfully with mango.

LEMON PUDDING CAKE

This bright, lemony cake might truly be magic. I know what you're thinking: The ingredients are basic pantry staples, not necessarily things found in a magic potion. But put them together following this method and these everyday ingredients separate during baking into two distinct layers of cake and pudding, both tart with lemon flavor and delightful in their own rights. I'm sure culinary scientists could offer a perfectly logical explanation, but we all know that culinary science is just another way to say magic, right?

PREP TIME: **15 minutes**

COOK TIME: **45 minutes to 1 hour**

EQUIPMENT: **8-inch square or round cake pan, whisk, electric mixer**

½ cup (1 stick) unsalted butter, melted, plus more for preparing the baking dish
4 eggs, at room temperature, separated
¾ cup sugar
1 teaspoon vanilla extract
¾ cup all-purpose flour
Zest of 1 lemon
¼ cup freshly squeezed lemon juice
1¾ cups low-fat or whole milk, slightly warmed
Powdered sugar, for dusting

1. Preheat the oven to 325°F.

2. Grease an 8-inch cake pan with butter.

3. In a large bowl, using an electric mixer, whip the egg whites until stiff peaks form.

4. In another large bowl, whisk the egg yolks and sugar until the mixture lightens.

5. Add the melted butter and vanilla and beat for 1 to 2 minutes more.

6. Add the flour and mix until it is fully incorporated.

7. Whisk in the lemon zest and juice.

8. While whisking or beating continuously, add the milk.

9. Gently fold in the egg whites, about ⅓ at a time, until they are mostly incorporated but bits of white are still visible. Transfer the batter to the prepared pan and bake for 45 minutes to 1 hour until the top is firm to the touch.

10. Remove from the oven and let the cake cool completely.

11. Dust the top with powdered sugar, and serve at room temperature. Cover any leftovers with plastic wrap and refrigerate for up to 3 days.

Ingredient tip: For a more pronounced lemon flavor, reduce the milk quantity slightly and replace it with additional freshly squeezed lemon juice.

CHOCOLATE BROWNIE PUDDING CAKE

Serves 6 to 8

Like the Magic Lemon Pudding Cake recipe (page 44), this recipe seems like it won't work. The batter is so runny you'll think it won't bake into a cake, and yet it does! Not only that, but it bakes into distinct layers of cake and pudding. And this version packs deep, rich chocolate flavor. Prepare to be amazed.

PREP TIME: **15 minutes**

COOK TIME: **1 hour**

EQUIPMENT: **8-inch square or round cake pan, whisk, electric mixer**

½ cup (1 stick) unsalted butter, melted, plus more for preparing the pan

¼ cup plus 3 tablespoons all-purpose flour, plus more for preparing the pan

4 eggs, at room temperature, separated

1 tablespoon water

1 teaspoon vanilla extract

Pinch salt

¼ cup plus 2 tablespoons unsweetened cocoa powder

2 cups low-fat or whole milk, slightly warmed

1 teaspoon vinegar

¾ cup powdered sugar

1. Preheat the oven to 325°F.

2. Grease an 8-inch cake pan with butter and dust with flour.

3. In a large bowl, whisk the egg yolks with the water until the eggs become creamy and light.

4. Add the melted butter, vanilla, and salt and beat until the mixture is light and fluffy.

5. Add the flour and cocoa powder in 3 batches, mixing after each addition until thoroughly incorporated.

6. Add the milk, a little at a time, mixing thoroughly after each addition.

7. In another large bowl, with a handheld mixer or whisk, whip the egg whites and vinegar until stiff peaks form. Add a scoop of the whipped egg whites to the chocolate mixture and gently fold it in.

8. Add a scoop of the chocolate mixture to the egg whites and gently fold to combine. Continue adding the chocolate mixture a little at a time to the egg white mixture, gently folding it in. Transfer the batter to the prepared pan and bake for about 1 hour until the cake is mostly set, but still slightly jiggly in the center.

9. Remove from the oven and set the pan on a wire rack to cool completely before slicing and serving. Cover any leftovers with plastic wrap and refrigerate for up to 3 days.

Technique tip: This cake batter is very thin, so mixing it by hand is recommended, as an electric mixer is likely to splatter. You'll want an electric mixer (either handheld or stand, or a whisk) to whip the egg whites, though, since that's the quickest way to get the stiff peaks you need here.

CREAMY
VANILLA BEAN POTS DE CRÈME

—⊱ Serves 8 ⊰—

These creamy little pots of custard, speckled with tiny vanilla bean seeds, are decadent, but simple to make. Cooking them in a water bath is key to making them creamy, smooth, and luxurious. They are perfectly lovely on their own, but a dollop of sweetened whipped cream on top certainly wouldn't hurt.

PREP TIME: **15 minutes**

COOK TIME: **25 to 30 minutes**

CHILLING TIME: **4 hours**

EQUIPMENT: **Medium saucepan, whisk, large baking dish, 8 (4-ounce) ramekins, fine-mesh sieve**

2 cups heavy (whipping) cream
½ cup whole milk
¼ teaspoon salt
1 vanilla bean, split lengthwise
6 egg yolks
¼ cup sugar
Lightly sweetened whipped cream, for serving (optional)

1. Preheat the oven to 300°F.

2. Place 8 (4-ounce) ramekins in a large baking dish.

3. In a medium saucepan set over medium heat, whisk the cream, milk, and salt.

4. Scrape the seeds from the inside of the vanilla bean into the cream, and then add the pod. Heat for about 4 minutes, stirring occasionally, until the mixture simmers.

5. Meanwhile, in a large bowl, whisk the egg yolks and sugar for about 4 minutes until the mixture becomes pale. While whisking continuously, add the hot cream mixture to the yolk mixture in a thin, slow stream. Continue whisking until the mixture is smooth. Strain it through a fine-mesh sieve into a large bowl or pitcher.

6. Ladle or pour the mixture into the ramekins, dividing evenly. Add enough hot water to the baking dish so it comes about halfway up the sides of the ramekins. Carefully transfer the baking dish to the oven and bake for 25 to 30 minutes until set around the edges, but still jiggly in the center.

7. Remove the baking dish from the oven and let the custards cool in the water bath for 5 minutes. Transfer the ramekins to a wire rack to cool completely. Refrigerate for at least 4 hours to chill. Serve chilled, topped with whipped cream (if using). Cover any leftovers with plastic wrap and refrigerate for up to 3 days.

Make-ahead tip: The pots de crème can be made up to 3 days in advance. Refrigerate, tightly covered.

ESPRESSO PANNA COTTA

⊱— Serves 4 —⊰

Panna cotta is the Italian answer to the French pots de crème. It's a creamy custard-like dessert that's thickened with gelatin. You can flavor it however you like—with chocolate, berries, vanilla bean, or (my favorite) espresso powder.

PREP TIME: **15 minutes**

COOK TIME: **5 minutes**

CHILLING TIME: **4 hours**

EQUIPMENT: **Small saucepan, 4 (6-ounce) ramekins**

1 cup whole milk

1 tablespoon unflavored
    powdered gelatin

3 cups heavy (whipping) cream

½ cup sugar

2 tablespoons instant espresso powder

Pinch salt

Dark chocolate shavings,
    for garnish (optional)

1. In a small saucepan, add the milk and sprinkle the gelatin over it. Let sit for 5 minutes. Place the pan over medium heat and gently heat for about 2 minutes, stirring frequently, until the gelatin dissolves.

2. Stir in the cream, sugar, espresso powder, and salt. Turn the heat to low and continue to heat for about 3 minutes more, just until the sugar dissolves. Spoon the mixture into 4 (6-ounce) ramekins or custard cups, dividing equally. Cover and refrigerate, stirring once or twice during the first hour of chilling. Let chill for at least 4 hours.

3. Serve chilled, garnished with chocolate shavings (if using). Refrigerate any leftovers (see tip).

Make-ahead tip: Panna cotta can be kept refrigerated for up to 3 days. Store tightly covered with plastic wrap and serve chilled.

STRAWBERRY CLAFOUTIS

— Serves 6 —

Clafoutis is one of my favorite desserts to serve guests, and I'm
the first to admit that one reason is its French name sounds
super fancy. It is also delicious and incredibly easy to make—
as simple as pouring a pancake-like batter over fresh fruit
and baking it. The result is a creamy, sweet dessert that is a
cross between a custard and a thick pancake. It is traditionally
made with cherries, but I love this strawberry version.

PREP TIME: **15 minutes**

COOK TIME: **30 minutes**

EQUIPMENT: **9-inch round baking
dish or pie dish, whisk**

3 tablespoons unsalted butter, melted,
   plus more for preparing the pan
½ cup all-purpose flour
¼ cup plus 2 tablespoons sugar
Pinch salt
3 eggs
Finely grated zest of 1 lemon
¼ cup plus 2 tablespoons
   low-fat or whole milk
3 cups halved or quartered fresh
   strawberries (about 1½ pints)
Powdered sugar, for garnish

1. Preheat the oven to 350°F.

2. Generously grease a 9-inch round
baking dish or pie dish with butter.

3. In a large bowl, whisk the flour, sugar,
and salt.

4. Add the eggs, melted butter, and lemon
zest. Whisk until smooth.

5. Add the milk and continue whisking for
about 3 minutes more until the mixture is
smooth and light.

6. Arrange the strawberries in an even
layer in the bottom of the prepared dish and
pour the batter over the top. Bake for about
30 minutes until the top is golden and the
center is set.

7. Remove from the oven and let cool for
a few minutes. Dust with powdered sugar,
slice into wedges, and serve immediately.
Cover any leftovers with plastic wrap and
refrigerate for up to 3 days.

Substitution tip: You can use just about any
fruit you like. In addition to berries, stone
fruits work especially well. Try cherries for a
classic version or use peaches or nectarines.

KEY LIME MOUSSE PIE CUPS

※— Serves 10 —※

With a crunchy graham cracker crust and a tangy, creamy mousse filling, these no-bake pie cups will satisfy any pie craving with far less work than the traditional version. These make a refreshing dessert for a warm summer evening. For a fun picnic dish, make them in small Mason jars, cap them, and bring them along in a cooler stocked with plenty of ice to keep them cold.

PREP TIME: **15 minutes**

CHILLING TIME: **1 hour**

EQUIPMENT: **10 (4-ounce) ramekins or custard cups, electric mixer**

⅔ cup graham cracker crumbs

2 teaspoons sugar

2 tablespoons unsalted butter, melted

2 cups cold heavy (whipping) cream

1 (14-ounce) can sweetened
    condensed milk

½ cup freshly squeezed key lime juice
    (from about 14 key limes)

Lime zest (optional)

1. In a small bowl, combine the graham cracker crumbs, sugar, and melted butter. Stir to mix well. Divide the mixture equally among 10 (4-ounce) ramekins or custard cups.

2. In a large bowl, using an electric mixer, whip the cream until stiff peaks form.

3. In another small bowl, whisk the sweetened condensed milk and lime juice. Gently fold the lime juice mixture into the whipped cream until incorporated. Spoon the mixture into the ramekins or custard cups on top of the graham cracker crust. Chill thoroughly, for at least 1 hour, and serve cold, garnished with the lime zest, if desired. Cover any leftovers with plastic wrap and refrigerate for up to 3 days.

Substitution tip: I love to make this with tiny, extra-tart key limes, but you can substitute regular limes if you like. Add extra flavor by including 1 tablespoon finely grated lime zest.

CLASSIC
CHOCOLATE MOUSSE

※ Serves 8 ※

This is another dessert I love to serve to guests, both because of its French pedigree and the fact that it is no fuss. Serve it in custard cups or martini glasses, topped with raspberries and whipped cream for a stunning presentation.

PREP TIME: **15 minutes**

CHILLING TIME: **4 hours**

EQUIPMENT: Small saucepan, electric mixer with whisk attachment

2 eggs

¼ cup sugar

2½ cups cold heavy (whipping) cream, divided

6 ounces semisweet chocolate, chopped

1. In a large bowl, using an electric mixer, beat together the eggs and sugar for 3 minutes.

2. In a small saucepan set over medium heat, bring 1 cup of cream to a simmer. Do not let it boil.

3. With the mixer running, add the hot cream to the egg mixture in a slow, steady stream until it is thoroughly incorporated. Transfer the egg and cream mixture to the saucepan and place it over low heat. Cook for about 5 minutes, stirring constantly, until the mixture thickens.

4. Remove the pan from the heat and add the chocolate. Stir until the chocolate is completely melted and incorporated. Refrigerate, covered, for at least 2 hours, stirring occasionally.

5. When the mixture is fully chilled, use an electric mixer with a whisk attachment to whip the remaining 1½ cups of cream until stiff peaks form. Add the whipped cream to the chilled chocolate mixture, gently folding, until it is fully incorporated and the mixture is smooth.

6. Cover with plastic wrap and refrigerate for at least 2 hours to chill. Serve chilled. Cover any leftovers with plastic wrap and refrigerate for up to 3 days.

Ingredient tip: Choose a semisweet chocolate that contains about 50 to 60 percent cocoa solids. Higher percentages produce a denser mousse.

PEACHES AND CREAM

※— Serves 4 —※

This gelatin-based dessert is loaded with the flavor of fresh, juicy peaches. Sour cream gives it richness, but it is refreshing enough to serve on a hot summer night. It can be made up to three days ahead, but I suggest you make the topping right before serving. It makes a perfect dish for entertaining.

PREP TIME: **10 minutes**
CHILLING TIME: **2 hours**
EQUIPMENT: **Blender or food processor, 4 (8-ounce) ramekins, custard cups, or wineglasses**

3 tablespoons cold water
2¼ teaspoons (1 envelope) unflavored gelatin
5 cups diced peaches, divided
½ cup plus 2 teaspoons sugar, divided
1 teaspoon vanilla extract
¾ cup sour cream

1. In a small microwave-safe bowl, stir together the water and gelatin. Microwave on high power for 20 seconds and stir. If the gelatin is not fully dissolved, return to the microwave for another 10 seconds on high power.

2. In a blender or food processor, combine 4 cups of peaches with ½ cup of the sugar and the vanilla. Process until smooth.

3. Add the sour cream and pulse to incorporate.

4. With the motor running on low, add the gelatin mixture in a slow steady stream. Divide the mixture evenly between 4 (8-ounce) ramekins, custard cups, or wineglasses, cover, and refrigerate for at least 2 hours, until set.

5. Before serving, in a small bowl, toss together the remaining 1 cup of diced peaches with the remaining 2 teaspoons of sugar and let macerate for about 2 minutes. Top each serving with some of the diced peaches and serve immediately. Cover any leftovers with plastic wrap and refrigerate for up to 3 days.

Substitution tip: For a different spin on this dish, substituted diced fresh strawberries for the peaches.

RASPBERRY PIE SQUARES

※ Makes 16 squares ※

A sweet-tart raspberry filling swirled with a sweetened cream cheese mixture and set over a graham cracker crust makes these dessert squares irresistible. Serve them as dessert for a summer barbecue or take them along on a picnic—put the covered pan in a cooler and slice into bars just before serving.

PREP TIME: 20 minutes

COOKING TIME: 10 minutes

CHILLING TIME: 3 hours, 30 minutes

EQUIPMENT: 8-inch square baking pan, blender or food processor

FOR THE CRUST

1½ cups finely ground graham cracker crumbs (from about 9 graham crackers)

⅓ cup sugar

6 tablespoons (¾ stick) unsalted butter, melted

FOR THE FILLING

2 tablespoons water

2¼ teaspoons (1 envelope) unflavored gelatin

3 cups fresh raspberries, divided

½ cup sugar

¼ cup cream cheese, at room temperature

2 tablespoons low-fat or whole milk

1 tablespoon powdered sugar

TO MAKE THE CRUST

1. Preheat the oven to 375°F.

2. In a medium bowl, stir together the graham cracker crumbs, sugar, and butter until well combined. Press the mixture into the bottom of an 8-inch baking pan in an even layer. Bake for about 7 minutes until lightly browned.

3. Remove from the oven and let cool.

TO MAKE THE FILLING

1. Put the water in a small bowl and sprinkle the gelatin over it. Let rest, stirring occasionally, until the gelatin fully dissolves. Prepare an ice bath by filling a large bowl with water and ice.

2. Meanwhile, in a blender or food processor, purée all but ½ cup of the raspberries until smooth. Transfer the purée to a medium saucepan set over medium heat.

3. Add the sugar and bring to a boil.

4. Add the gelatin mixture and cook for about 1 minute, stirring. Transfer the raspberry mixture to a medium bowl and set the bowl in the ice bath. Transfer the ice bath with the filling mixture to the refrigerator and chill for about 30 minutes, stirring once in a while with a rubber spatula, until the mixture is cool and thick.

5. While the raspberry mixture chills, in a medium bowl, combine the cream cheese, milk, and powdered sugar and, using an electric mixer or wooden spoon, beat until very smooth.

6. Spread the chilled raspberry filling over the prepared graham cracker crust and spoon the cream cheese mixture on top, placing dollops all over. Drag a knife through the cream cheese mixture to swirl it with the raspberry mixture. Top with the reserved raspberries. Refrigerate for about 3 hours, until fully set. Cut into 16 squares and serve chilled. Cover any leftovers with plastic wrap and refrigerate for up to 3 days.

Substitution tip: This sweet dessert can be made with other fruits as well. I love it with blueberries, strawberries, or blackberries.

Chapter Four

ICE CREAM, SORBET

& OTHER FROZEN TREATS

Left (clockwise from top-right): Easy No-Cook Vanilla Ice Cream (page 60),
Dark Chocolate Ice Cream (page 61), and Roasted Strawberry Ice Cream (page 62)

EASY NO-COOK
VANILLA ICE CREAM

—※— Serves 8 —※—

For this classic vanilla ice cream, you don't need to go through the elaborate process of making a custard base or using an ice cream maker. Just mix together the ingredients, chill them, and freeze them in the freezer. The key to making a smooth, creamy ice cream without an ice cream maker is to stir it vigorously and frequently as it freezes to break up the hard ice crystals that form.

PREP TIME: **10 minutes**

CHILLING AND FREEZING TIME: **4 hours**

EQUIPMENT: **Freezer-safe storage container**

1 cup whole milk
¾ cup granulated sugar
Pinch salt
2 cups heavy (whipping) cream
1 tablespoon vanilla extract

1. In a medium bowl, combine the milk, sugar, and salt. Whisk, or use an electric mixer to beat, for about 3 minutes until the sugar dissolves.

2. Add the cream and vanilla and stir to mix. Refrigerate for at least 1 hour.

3. Pour the mixture into a freezer-safe storage container, cover with plastic wrap, and freeze for about 45 minutes before checking on it the first time. As soon as it begins to freeze around the edges, mix it vigorously with a whisk, spatula, wooden spoon, or ideally, a handheld electric mixer or immersion blender. Continue to freeze, mixing it every 30 minutes, until it is fully frozen, about 3 hours total.

4. Keep frozen until ready to serve.

Technique tip: If you have an electric ice cream maker, by all means use it. Freeze the container for at least 24 hours before starting your ice cream. After step 2, transfer the mixture to the ice cream maker and freeze according to the manufacturer's instructions.

DARK CHOCOLATE ICE CREAM

⸺ ❈ Serves 8 ❈ ⸺

This rich, dark chocolate ice cream will satisfy even the biggest chocolate fiend. If you want to make it even more intense, add crumbled brownies to the mix before freezing. Serve it on its own or with fresh raspberries or strawberries, topped with a dollop of whipped cream, or sandwiched between two chocolate chip cookies.

PREP TIME: **20 minutes**
CHILLING AND FREEZING TIME: **5 hours**
EQUIPMENT: **Freezer-safe storage container**

8 ounces semisweet chocolate, finely chopped
1 cup whole milk
2 cups heavy (whipping) cream
¾ cup granulated sugar
Pinch salt
1 teaspoon vanilla extract

1. In a medium microwave-safe bowl, combine the chocolate and milk. Microwave at 50 percent power, in 30-second intervals, stirring in between, until the chocolate melts and the mixture is smooth. Let cool for several minutes.

2. Meanwhile, in another medium bowl, combine the cream, sugar, and salt. Whisk, or use an electric mixer to beat, for about 3 minutes until the sugar dissolves.

3. Add the vanilla and the chocolate mixture and stir to combine well. Refrigerate for at least 2 hours until fully chilled.

4. Pour the mixture into a freezer-safe storage container, cover with plastic wrap, and freeze for about 45 minutes before checking on it the first time. As soon as it begins to freeze around the edges, mix it vigorously with a whisk, spatula, wooden spoon, or ideally, a handheld electric mixer or immersion blender. Continue to freeze, mixing it every 30 minutes, until it is fully frozen, about 3 hours total.

5. Keep frozen until ready to serve.

Ingredient tip: Use a chocolate with a high percentage of cocoa solids (60 percent or above) for intense chocolate flavor.

ROASTED STRAWBERRY ICE CREAM

— Serves 8 —

Roasting strawberries caramelizes their sugars, deepening and intensifying the flavor. This ice cream is luscious on its own, but drizzled with hot fudge sauce it is the stuff dreams are made of. You can substitute just about any other fruit for the strawberries. Roasted peaches, nectarines, or cherries would be just as good.

PREP TIME: **15 minutes**

COOK TIME: **35 to 40 minutes**

CHILLING AND FREEZING TIME: **4 hours, 30 minutes**

EQUIPMENT: **Freezer-safe storage container, a large baking dish with 2-inch sides**

1 pound fresh strawberries, cored and diced

3 tablespoons mild-flavored honey

1 cup whole milk

¾ cup sugar

Pinch salt

2 cups heavy (whipping) cream

1 teaspoon vanilla extract

1. Preheat the oven to 375°F.

2. Arrange the berries in a single layer in a large baking dish with 2-inch sides. Toss the berries with the honey. Roast for 35 to 40 minutes, stirring occasionally, until the juices have run out and thickened. Scrape the roasted fruit and all the juices into a bowl and refrigerate for at least 30 minutes.

3. In a medium bowl, combine the milk, sugar, and salt. Whisk, or use an electric mixer to beat, for about 3 minutes until the sugar dissolves.

4. Add the cream, vanilla, and roasted strawberries and stir to mix. Refrigerate for at least 1 hour until fully chilled.

5. Pour the mixture into a freezer-safe storage container, cover with plastic wrap, and freeze for about 45 minutes before checking on it the first time. As soon as it begins to freeze around the edges, mix it vigorously with a whisk, spatula, wooden spoon, or ideally, a handheld electric mixer or immersion blender. Continue to freeze, mixing it every 30 minutes, until it is fully frozen, about 3 hours total.

6. Keep frozen until ready to serve.

Make-ahead tip: You can make the roasted strawberries, the ice cream base mixture, or both up to 2 days ahead. Refrigerate until you're ready to freeze the ice cream.

BUTTERSCOTCH ICE CREAM

⋯— Serves 8 —⋯

People often assume that, because of its name, butterscotch either originated in Scotland or contains Scotch whisky. Neither is true. "Scotch" here is probably derived from the word *scorch*. It's scorched, or cooked, butter and brown sugar that creates the distinctive taste. Serve a scoop of this on top of Peach Upside-Down Cake (page 92) for a fabulous summer dessert.

PREP TIME: **20 minutes**

COOK TIME: **5 minutes**

CHILLING AND FREEZING TIME: **5 hours**

EQUIPMENT: **Freezer-safe storage container**

1 cup packed light brown sugar

2 tablespoons unsalted butter

2 cups heavy (whipping) cream, divided

2 teaspoons vanilla extract

1 cup whole milk

¼ teaspoon kosher salt

1. In a medium saucepan set over medium heat, combine the brown sugar and butter. Cook for about 5 minutes, stirring frequently with a silicone spatula, scraping the melted sugar from the bottom of the pan to prevent burning, until the butter and sugar are melted and smooth.

2. While whisking constantly, carefully add 1 cup of heavy cream, whisking for about 4 minutes until the mixture is smooth.

3. Remove the pan from the heat and stir in the vanilla.

4. In a medium bowl, combine the milk, salt, and remaining 1 cup of heavy cream. Whisk, or use an electric mixer to beat, for about 3 minutes until the sugar dissolves.

5. Add the butterscotch mixture and stir to mix well. Refrigerate for at least 2 hours, until fully chilled.

6. Pour the mixture into a freezer-safe storage container, cover with plastic wrap, and freeze for about 45 minutes before checking on it the first time. As soon as it begins to freeze around the edges, mix it vigorously with a whisk, spatula, wooden spoon, or ideally, a handheld electric mixer or immersion blender. Continue to freeze, mixing it every 30 minutes, until it is fully frozen, about 3 hours total.

7. Keep frozen until ready to serve.

Ingredient tip : For added flavor, add 1 tablespoon whiskey along with the vanilla in step 2.

ORANGE SHERBET

— Serves 8 —

Sherbet is differentiated from ice cream by the use of whole milk and fruit juice in place of cream. This one bursts with orange flavor. As with the ice cream recipes I've shared (see pages 60 to 65), you can use an ice cream maker to freeze this if you have one available.

PREP TIME: **10 minutes**

CHILLING AND FREEZING TIME: **5 hours**

EQUIPMENT: **Freezer-safe** storage container

½ cup sugar

½ cup frozen orange juice concentrate, thawed or partially thawed

2 cups freshly squeezed orange juice

1½ cups whole milk

2 tablespoons freshly squeezed lemon juice

1 tablespoon vanilla extract

¼ teaspoon salt

1. In a medium bowl, stir together the sugar, orange juice concentrate, orange juice, milk, lemon juice, vanilla, and salt until well combined and smooth. Refrigerate the mixture for at least 2 hours until fully chilled.

2. Pour the mixture into a freezer-safe storage container, cover with plastic wrap, and freeze for about 45 minutes before checking on it the first time. As soon as it begins to freeze around the edges, mix it vigorously with a whisk, spatula, wooden spoon, or ideally, a handheld electric mixer or immersion blender. Continue to freeze, mixing it every 30 minutes until it is fully frozen, about 3 hours total.

3. Store in the freezer until ready to serve.

Ingredient tip: Alcohol keeps ice cream from forming hard ice crystals, so adding a bit to your mix will give you a smooth, creamy texture. In this recipe, a few tablespoons of orange-flavored liqueur, such as Cointreau, will add extra orange flavor as well.

CHERRY-VANILLA FROZEN YOGURT

Serves 8

Tart-sweet cherries, creamy vanilla, and rich yogurt combine to make a sublime frozen treat in this recipe. Because I have a hard time thinking of cherry desserts without also thinking of chocolate, I love this frozen yogurt sandwiched between two chocolate wafer cookies. It's also great with hot fudge sauce drizzled over the top just before devouring.

PREP TIME: **20 minutes**

CHILLING TIME: **3 hours**

EQUIPMENT: **Medium saucepan, blender, freezer-safe storage container**

3 cups pitted fresh cherries

¾ cup sugar

2 tablespoons freshly squeezed lemon juice

1½ cups full-fat plain yogurt

¼ cup whole milk

1 tablespoon vanilla extract

1. In a medium saucepan set over medium-high heat, combine the cherries, sugar, and lemon juice, stirring until the mixture simmers and the sugar fully dissolves. Remove from the heat and let cool for 10 minutes.

2. Transfer the cherry mixture to a blender and process until smooth.

3. Add the yogurt, milk, and vanilla. Pulse to mix well. Pour the mixture into a freezer-safe storage container, cover with plastic wrap, and freeze for about 45 minutes before checking on it the first time. As soon as it begins to freeze around the edges, mix it vigorously with a whisk, spatula, wooden spoon, or ideally, a handheld electric mixer or immersion blender. Continue to freeze, mixing it every 30 minutes, until it is fully frozen, about 3 hours total.

4. Keep frozen until ready to serve.

Substitution tip: Use strawberries or blueberries instead of the cherries in this recipe.

DARK CHOCOLATE SORBET

— Serves 8 —

Chocoholics rejoice! Made with both cocoa powder and semisweet chocolate, this dairy-free frozen treat packs intense chocolate flavor. Top it with a dollop of whipped cream (whipped coconut cream if you want to keep it dairy free) or a handful of raspberries for a delightful and refreshing dessert.

PREP TIME: **15 minutes**

CHILLING AND FREEZING TIME:

5 to 6 hours

EQUIPMENT: **Freezer-safe storage container**

1 cup sugar

¾ cup unsweetened Dutch process cocoa powder

Pinch salt

6 ounces semisweet chocolate, finely chopped

1 teaspoon vanilla extract

1. In a large saucepan over medium-high heat, whisk the sugar, cocoa powder, salt, and 1¼ cups water. Bring to a boil and let it cook for about 45 seconds, whisking constantly. Remove from the heat and immediately add the chocolate. Stir until the chocolate completely melts and the mixture is smooth.

2. Stir in the vanilla and 1 cup water. Refrigerate for at least 2 hours until fully chilled.

3. Pour the mixture into a freezer-safe storage container, cover with plastic wrap, and freeze for about 45 minutes before checking on it the first time. As soon as it begins to freeze around the edges, mix it vigorously with a whisk, spatula, wooden spoon, or ideally, a handheld electric mixer or immersion blender. Continue to freeze, mixing it every 30 minutes, until it is fully frozen, 3 to 4 hours total.

4. Keep frozen until ready to serve.

Ingredient tip: Dutch process cocoa powder differs from natural cocoa powder in that it has been washed with a solution that neutralizes the chocolate's natural acidity, giving it a smoother, earthier flavor than natural cocoa powder, which tends to have more of a citrusy finish. In some recipes, Dutch process cocoa powder is used because the lower acidity keeps it from reacting with alkaline leavening agents such as baking soda, but here it is simply a matter of flavor.

TANGY
LEMON SORBET

⁓ Serves 8 ⁓

I love lemon sorbet on a hot day. Its bright, citrusy flavor is so refreshing. Many homemade sorbet recipes are disappointing because the juice just freezes into a solid block of ice, but this one maintains a consistency you can easily scoop, even after several days in the freezer. That's thanks to the tablespoon of vodka. You won't taste it in the finished sorbet, but it keeps the liquid from freezing solid.

PREP TIME: **20 minutes**

CHILLING AND FREEZING TIME: **5 to 6 hours**

EQUIPMENT: **Freezer-safe storage container**

2 cups light corn syrup

1½ cups cold water

1 cup freshly squeezed lemon juice (from about 6 lemons)

1 tablespoon vodka

Zest of 1 lemon

½ teaspoon salt

1. In a medium bowl, whisk the corn syrup, water, lemon juice, vodka, lemon zest, and salt until smooth and well combined. Refrigerate for at least 2 hours until fully chilled.

2. Pour the mixture into a freezer-safe storage container, cover with plastic wrap, and freeze for about 45 minutes before checking on it the first time. As soon as it begins to freeze around the edges, mix it vigorously with a whisk, spatula, wooden spoon, or ideally, a handheld electric mixer or immersion blender. Continue to freeze, mixing it every 30 minutes, until it is fully frozen, 3 to 4 hours total.

3. Keep frozen until ready to serve.

Substitution tip: Use any citrus juice you like here. Try lime or orange, but taste and adjust the corn syrup quantity depending on the sweetness of your juice. You might need a bit more corn syrup if using lime juice, or a bit less if using orange juice.

TROPICAL ICE POPS

Makes 10 ice pops

These ice pops explode with bright, refreshing flavor and are made from just a few ingredients. Eating these makes me feel like I'm on a beach on a tropical island. And anything that makes me feel that way is a winner in my book. I suspect you'll be replenishing your freezer supply frequently during the summer months.

PREP TIME: **5 minutes**

FREEZING TIME: **6 hours**

EQUIPMENT: **Blender, 10 ice pop molds or small paper cups and ice pop sticks**

4 cups frozen pineapple
1 cup canned coconut milk
2 teaspoons vanilla extract
2 tablespoons sugar, as needed

1. In a blender, purée the pineapple, coconut milk, and vanilla until smooth. Taste and add sugar as needed, blending to incorporate it.

2. Pour the mixture into 10 ice pop molds or paper cups and freeze for about 45 minutes before adding the sticks. Freeze for at least 6 hours until frozen solid. Keep frozen.

Substitution tip : For variety, substitute other tropical fruits, like frozen banana or mango, for some or all of the pineapple.

WATERMELON ICE POPS

⟶ Makes 10 ice pops ⟶

These ice pops are just adorable. They take a little extra work since they have to be frozen in two stages, but the hands-on time is minimal, and the end result is totally worth it. The chocolate chips are a delightful surprise and they look like watermelon seeds!

PREP TIME: **20 minutes**
FREEZING TIME: **7 hours**
EQUIPMENT: **Blender, 10 ice pop molds** or small paper cups and ice pop sticks

3 ½ cups cubed seedless watermelon
5 tablespoons sugar, divided
1 tablespoon freshly squeezed
    lemon juice
1 tablespoon mini chocolate chips
10 kiwi fruits, peeled and diced

1. In a blender, combine the watermelon with 2 tablespoons of sugar and the lemon juice and blend until smooth. Pour the mixture into 10 ice pop molds, filling the molds two-thirds full.

2. Add a few chocolate chips to each mold, pressing them down into the juice with one of the ice pop sticks or a skewer. Freeze for at least 4 hours.

3. Meanwhile, in a blender, combine the kiwi with the remaining 3 tablespoons of sugar and blend until smooth. Strain

the mixture through a fine-mesh sieve to remove the seeds. Chill for at least 30 minutes.

4. Once the watermelon layer is frozen, remove the molds from the freezer and top off each mold with 2 tablespoons of kiwi mixture and insert the sticks. Return to the freezer and freeze for at least 3 hours more until solid.

Topping tip: These are even cuter with a layer of creamy white separating the watermelon flesh from the rind. Use ½ cup coconut milk mixed with 1 ½ tablespoons sugar, and spoon 1 tablespoon into each ice pop mold after the watermelon portion has been frozen. Halve the quantities for the kiwi mixture and add 1 tablespoon to the molds after the coconut milk portion has been in the freezer for 3 hours.

ESPRESSO FROZEN YOGURT POPS

⋇— Makes 10 frozen yogurt pops —⋇

This ice pop recipe makes creamy espresso-flavored frozen pops that will perk you up while they cool you down. Because of the coffee, these are a grown-up treat, but they're so sweet and smooth that I'm willing to bet your kids will beg for them, too.

PREP TIME: **5 minutes**

FREEZING TIME: **6 hours, 45 minutes**

EQUIPMENT: **10 ice pop molds or small paper cups and ice pop sticks**

3 cups vanilla yogurt

⅔ cup low-fat or whole milk

½ cup sugar

2 tablespoons instant espresso powder

1. In a large pitcher, stir together the yogurt, milk, sugar, and espresso powder until well combined. Pour the mixture into 10 ice pop molds.

2. Freeze for at least 45 minutes before inserting the sticks. Freeze for at least 6 hours until frozen solid. Keep frozen until ready to serve

Substitution tip: Made with full-fat yogurt and milk, these ice pops are super creamy, but you can use low-fat versions if you prefer a healthier treat.

BLACKBERRY FROZEN YOGURT SWIRL POPS

Makes 10 frozen yogurt pops

These swirly, creamy blackberry frozen yogurt pops are beautiful.
I love the intense color of the blackberries almost as much as I love
the way their sweetness melds with the creamy yogurt. This is another
treat that gets stocked regularly in my freezer over the summer.

PREP TIME: **10 minutes**

COOK TIME: **10 minutes**

CHILLING AND FREEZING TIME: **6 hours,
30 minutes**

EQUIPMENT: **Medium saucepan, blender,
10 ice pop molds or small paper cups
and ice pop sticks**

2 cups fresh blackberries,
   halved if large
1 tablespoon freshly squeezed
   lemon juice
½ cup plus 2 tablespoons
   sugar, divided
1½ cups plain yogurt

1. In a medium bowl, toss the berries with
the lemon juice and 2 tablespoons of sugar.
Set aside.

2. In a medium saucepan set over medium-
high heat, combine ½ cup water with the
remaining ½ cup of sugar and cook, stirring,
until the water boils and the sugar dissolves.
Lower the heat and simmer for 5 minutes
more until the mixture is syrupy. Remove
from the heat and transfer to a storage
container or pitcher. Refrigerate for about
30 minutes until chilled.

CONTINUED →

3. In another medium bowl, whisk the yogurt with the chilled syrup.

4. In a blender, purée the berries until mostly smooth. Strain through a fine-mesh sieve into a bowl to remove the seeds.

5. To make the ice pops, fill the molds with alternating layers of yogurt mixture and berry purée until the molds are full. Leave about ½ inch at the top to allow for expansion as they freeze. Use an ice pop stick, skewer, or chopstick to gently swirl together the two mixtures. Transfer the pops to the freezer for about 45 minutes before inserting the sticks. Continue to freeze for at least 6 hours until frozen. Keep frozen until ready to serve.

Substitution tip : These are particularly stunning made with blackberries, but use whatever berries you like or have an abundance of. Strawberries, raspberries, or blueberries would all be great.

CLASSIC
ICE CREAM SANDWICHES
WITH CHOCOLATE COOKIES

⁕ Makes 12 ice cream sandwiches ⁕

Biting into a classic ice cream sandwich—creamy vanilla ice cream bound by two soft chocolate cookies—brings me instantly back to childhood summers. I can practically feel the ice cream dripping down my arm as the summer heat melts it faster than I can eat it. This recipe brings the childhood memory to life. You can use any flavor ice cream you like (the Roasted Strawberry Ice Cream, page 62, would be divine), but I'll stick to classic vanilla here, like the Easy No-Cook Vanilla Ice Cream (page 60), for old times' sake.

PREP TIME: **30 minutes**

COOK TIME: **10 to 12 minutes**

CHILLING AND FREEZING TIME: **1 hour, 30 minutes**

EQUIPMENT: **9-by-13-inch baking pan, electric mixer**

½ gallon vanilla ice cream, slightly softened

2⅔ cups all-purpose flour, plus more for the work surface

⅔ cup plus ¼ cup unsweetened cocoa powder

¾ teaspoon salt

1¼ cups (2½ sticks) unsalted butter

1 cup sugar

2 egg yolks

2 teaspoons vanilla extract

1. Line a 9-by-13-inch baking pan with parchment paper (use enough paper so it hangs over the sides). Transfer the softened ice cream to the prepared pan and use a rubber spatula to spread it into an even layer. Cover with plastic wrap and freeze for at least 1 hour until frozen solid.

2. Preheat the oven to 350°F.

3. Line 2 baking sheets with parchment paper.

4. Meanwhile, in a medium bowl sift together the flour, cocoa powder, and salt.

5. In a large bowl, using a handheld electric mixer or a stand mixer at medium speed, cream together the butter and sugar for about 1 minute until creamy and lightened in color.

CONTINUED →

6. Add the egg yolks and vanilla and mix to incorporate.

7. Add the dry ingredients and mix until just combined. Split the dough into 2 equal pieces and pat each piece into a 5-inch square. Wrap the squares in plastic wrap and refrigerate for 30 minutes.

8. When the dough is thoroughly chilled, turn it out onto a lightly floured surface and roll each square into an 8-by-12-inch rectangle. Cut each rectangle into 6 (2-by-8-inch) strips. Halve each strip widthwise to make 24 (2-by-4-inch) rectangles. Transfer the cookies to the prepared sheets, and using a skewer or chopstick, make 2 lines of holes running down the length of each cookie. Bake for 10 to 12 minutes until firm.

9. Remove from the oven and transfer the cookies to a wire rack to cool completely.

10. When the cookies are completely cooled, lift the ice cream out of the baking pan using the parchment paper. Trim the edges so they are straight, creating a straight-sided 8-by-12-inch rectangle. Cut the ice cream into 6 (2-by-8-inch) strips and halve each strip widthwise to make 12 (2-by-4-inch) rectangles.

11. Place each ice cream rectangle between 2 cookies and press together slightly. Serve immediately or wrap in parchment paper or plastic wrap and freeze.

Technique tip: The sandwiches can be served immediately or wrapped in parchment paper and frozen, up to 3 months. Left overnight in the freezer, the cookies soften a bit, making the sandwiches even better the day after they are made.

CHOCOLATE-HAZELNUT FUDGE POPS

Makes 6 ice pops

These fudge pops are easy to make with only about 10 minutes of hands-on time. The hardest part is waiting for them to freeze. Once frozen, you can remove them from the molds, refreeze them on a baking sheet, and stash them in a resealable plastic bag.

PREP TIME: **10 minutes**
FREEZING TIME: **6 hours**
EQUIPMENT: **Medium saucepan,
6 ice pop molds or small paper
cups and ice pop sticks**

1 cup whole milk
1 cup chocolate-hazelnut spread
   (like Nutella)
½ cup heavy (whipping) cream
2 tablespoons dark cocoa powder
1 teaspoon vanilla extract

1. In a medium saucepan set over low heat, stir together the milk, chocolate-hazelnut spread, cream, cocoa powder, and vanilla for 5 to 10 minutes until the chocolate-hazelnut spread is fully melted and the mixture is well combined. Remove from the heat and set aside to cool for about 10 minutes.

2. Pour the chocolate mixture into 6 ice pop molds or paper cups set on a sheet pan. Freeze for about 45 minutes before adding the sticks. Continue to freeze for at least 6 hours until completely frozen solid. Keep frozen until ready to serve.

Ingredient tip: You can make chocolate-hazelnut spread at home: Combine 1 cup raw hazelnuts, 2 teaspoons vanilla extract, 2 tablespoons cocoa powder, 6 tablespoons sugar, a pinch of salt, and ¼ cup milk in a food processor or blender. Process until very smooth. This recipe makes 1 cup, just enough for the fudge pops. Double the ingredients so you'll have some left over to spread on toast!

TIRAMISU ICE CREAM CAKE

⊰⊱— Serves 8 —⊰⊱

Tiramisu Ice Cream Cake is a fun spin on the classic Italian
dessert. Like the original, this version uses ladyfingers dipped
in coffee, but here the layers in between are made of coffee
ice cream instead of custard. A chocolate-cookie-crumb crust
anchors the whole thing and a dusting of chocolate or cocoa
powder over the top adds a nice hint of chocolate flavor.

PREP TIME: **30 minutes**
FREEZING TIME: **6 hours, 30 minutes**
EQUIPMENT: **9-inch springform pan**

Nonstick baking spray, for
   preparing the pan
25 chocolate wafer cookies, finely
   crushed, plus more for garnish
   (I prefer Nabisco Famous
   Chocolate Wafers)
2 tablespoons unsalted butter, melted
3 pints coffee ice cream, divided
1½ cups brewed espresso or
   strong coffee, cooled
30 soft ladyfingers, divided
1 cup heavy (whipping) cream
2 tablespoons sugar
¼ cup finely grated semisweet
   chocolate, or cocoa powder

1. Coat the inside of a 9-inch springform
pan with nonstick baking spray.

2. In a small bowl, stir together the cookie
crumbs and butter. Press the mixture into
the bottom of the prepared pan. Transfer
the pan to the freezer.

3. Let the ice cream sit on the countertop
at room temperature for about 15 minutes
until it softens. Transfer to a large bowl
and stir it until it softens into a spreadable
consistency.

4. Remove the pan from the freezer and spread ⅓ of the ice cream over the crust. Dip the ladyfingers into the coffee and arrange them in a single layer covering the layer of ice cream. Repeat twice more so you have 3 layers of ice cream separated by 3 layers of espresso-dipped ladyfingers. Cover with plastic wrap and return to the freezer for about 30 minutes.

5. In a large bowl, combine the cream and sugar, using a handheld electric mixer or a stand mixer to whip the ingredients until the cream holds soft peaks.

6. Remove the pan from the freezer again and spread the whipped cream over the top. Garnish with the shaved chocolate or cocoa powder, cover with plastic wrap, and return the pan to the freezer for at least 6 hours.

7. To serve, unmold the cake from the springform pan and slice it into wedges. Serve straight out of the freezer and keep any unused portion covered and frozen.

Substitution tip: Feel free to mix up the ice cream flavor here. You could use different flavors of ice cream (such as coffee, vanilla, and chocolate) for each of the 3 layers.

Chapter Five

CAKES & CUPCAKES

Left: White Chocolate–Raspberry Swirl Cheesecake (page 88)

STRAWBERRY SHORTCAKE

— Serves 6 —

Strawberry shortcake is one of the great simple pleasures in life. A lightly sweetened biscuit-like cake split and filled with fluffy whipped cream and sweet strawberries is perfect for a summer barbecue, or any other spring or summer celebration.

PREP TIME: **20 minutes**

COOK TIME: **18 to 20 minutes**

CHILLING AND COOLING TIME: **45 minutes**

EQUIPMENT: **8-inch square baking pan, electric mixer**

1½ pounds fresh strawberries, stemmed and quartered

½ cup sugar, divided

2 cups all-purpose flour

2 teaspoons baking powder

¾ teaspoon salt

¼ teaspoon baking soda

3 cups chilled heavy (whipping) cream, divided

1½ teaspoons vanilla extract

1. In a large bowl, toss the strawberries with 3 tablespoons of sugar. Refrigerate for at least 30 minutes to let the strawberries macerate.

2. Preheat the oven to 400°F.

3. In a medium bowl, stir together the flour, baking powder, baking soda, salt, and 2 tablespoons of sugar.

4. Add 1½ cups of cream and stir until just combined. Transfer the batter to an 8-inch square baking pan and bake for 18 to 20 minutes until golden brown.

5. Remove from the oven and invert the cake onto a wire rack to cool.

6. While the cake cools, make the whipped cream. Using a handheld electric mixer or a stand mixer, beat the remaining 1½ cups of cream with the remaining 3 tablespoons of sugar for about 3 minutes until the cream holds soft peaks.

7. Add the vanilla and beat to incorporate.

8. Once cooled, cut the cake into 6 rectangular pieces and split each horizontally. Put the bottom halves of the cake onto 6 serving plates and spoon some of the strawberries, along with the juice that has collected in the bowl, over them. Add a generous dollop of whipped cream and top with the cake tops. Serve immediately.

Make-ahead tip: The cake can be made up to 2 days in advance and stored, wrapped in plastic wrap, at room temperature. The whipped cream can be kept, covered, in the refrigerator for up to 2 days. Prepare the strawberries and assemble the cakes just before serving.

ESPRESSO ICEBOX CAKE

— Serves 8 —

Layers of chocolate wafers, rich, sweetened whipped cream combined with mascarpone cheese, and coffee liqueur turn into a delightful cake after chilling for several hours. This cake is ideal for summer birthday celebrations when you want a cake but don't want to heat up your kitchen.

PREP TIME: **20 minutes**

CHILLING AND FREEZING TIME: **9 hours**

EQUIPMENT: **10-inch springform pan, electric mixer**

3 cups chilled heavy (whipping) cream, divided

½ cup plus 1 tablespoon sugar, divided

1 cup (about 9 ounces) mascarpone cheese, at room temperature

¼ cup coffee liqueur, such as Kahlua

42 chocolate wafer cookies, divided (I prefer Nabisco Famous Chocolate Wafers)

1 tablespoon instant espresso powder

1. In a large bowl, using a handheld electric mixer or in a stand mixer, beat together 2 cups of cream with 6 tablespoons of sugar for about 3 minutes until the cream holds soft peaks.

2. With the mixer set on low speed, add the mascarpone and coffee liqueur. Mix to combine.

3. Spread 1¼ cups of the mascarpone mixture over the bottom of the springform pan in an even layer. Top with 14 chocolate wafers, slightly overlapping them as needed. Top the wafers with another 1¼ cups of mascarpone and another layer of 14 wafers. Top with the remaining mascarpone, smoothing the top with a spatula. Cover the pan and freeze for about 1 hour until the cake is firm. Transfer the cake to the refrigerator and chill for 8 hours or longer until the cookies are soft and the cake is set.

4. Crush the remaining wafers in a blender, food processor, or in a resealable plastic bag with a rolling pin.

5. In a medium bowl, using an electric mixer or a stand mixer set at medium speed, whip the remaining 1 cup of cream with the espresso powder and the remaining 3 tablespoons of sugar for about 3 minutes, just until the cream holds stiff peaks.

6. Unmold the cake from the pan, spread the espresso cream over the top and sides, and sprinkle the wafer crumbs over the top. Serve chilled.

Substitution tip: For a little variety, use chocolate chip cookies (a crispier kind) instead of the chocolate wafers. Either version will be gone before you know it.

WHITE CHOCOLATE-RASPBERRY SWIRL CHEESECAKE

Serves 10

Cheesecake—so rich, creamy, and lush—hardly needs dressing up, but this version is as visually stunning as it is delicious. Its intense white chocolate flavor and gorgeous swirls of sweet raspberry preserves make it the belle of the cheesecake ball. It definitely doesn't require any additional garnish, but a drizzle of dark chocolate sauce wouldn't hurt.

PREP TIME: **20 minutes**

COOK TIME: **35 to 40 minutes**

CHILLING TIME: **3 hours**

EQUIPMENT: **Electric mixer, 9-inch springform pan**

2 cups chocolate wafer cookie crumbs (I prefer Nabisco Famous Chocolate Wafers)

4 tablespoons (½ stick) unsalted butter, melted

2 (8-ounce) packages cream cheese, at room temperature

½ cup sugar

½ teaspoon vanilla extract

2 eggs

3 ounces white chocolate, melted

3 tablespoons raspberry preserves

1. Preheat the oven to 350°F.

2. In a small bowl, combine the cookie crumbs and melted butter. Press the mixture into the bottom and partway up the sides of a 9-inch springform pan.

3. In a medium bowl, using a handheld electric mixer or in a stand mixer, beat together the cream cheese, sugar, and vanilla.

4. Add the eggs and beat until just combined.

5. Stir in the white chocolate and pour the batter into the prepared crust.

6. Put the preserves in a small microwave-safe bowl and microwave at high power for about 20 seconds to melt. Using a small spoon, dollop the preserves on top of the cheesecake. Use the tip of a knife to drag and swirl the preserves through the batter. Bake for 35 to 40 minutes until the center is mostly set.

7. Remove from the oven and let cool. Refrigerate for at least 3 hours before serving.

Technique tip: Cheesecake needs lots of humidity to cook without cracking. Place a baking pan filled with water on the oven's bottom rack before preheating and leave it there while the cheesecake bakes.

BLACKBERRY CRUMB CAKE

— Serves 8 —

Blackberries grow like weeds where I live, but as far as I'm concerned, there's no such thing as too many. If you are lucky enough to find yourself with an abundance of them, bake this delectable crumb cake. It's perfect for a weekend brunch, with a cup of tea on a lazy afternoon, or as an after-dinner dessert.

PREP TIME: 10 minutes

COOK TIME: 45 minutes

EQUIPMENT: Electric mixer, 8-inch square or round cake pan

FOR THE TOPPING

½ cup old-fashioned rolled oats

½ cup packed brown sugar

¼ cup all-purpose flour

4 tablespoons (½ stick) cold unsalted butter

FOR THE CAKE

4 tablespoons (½ stick) unsalted butter, at room temperature, plus more for preparing the baking pan

1¾ cups all-purpose flour, plus more for preparing the baking pan

¾ cup sugar

1 egg

1 teaspoon vanilla extract

Zest of 1 lemon

2 teaspoons baking powder

½ teaspoon salt

½ cup low-fat or whole milk

2 heaping cups fresh blackberries, halved if large

TO MAKE THE CUPCAKES

1. Preheat the oven to 350°F.

2. Line a 12-cup muffin tin with paper liners.

3. In a large bowl, with a handheld electric mixer or in a stand mixer, cream together the butter and sugar on medium speed for about 3 minutes until the mixture becomes pale and fluffy.

4. Add the egg and beat on high speed to incorporate.

5. In a small bowl, stir together the cocoa powder, food coloring, and vanilla. Add this mixture to the batter and beat on medium speed to combine well.

6. With the mixer running on low speed, add the buttermilk and flour in alternating batches, beating to combine after each addition. Turn the mixer to high speed and beat until smooth.

7. Add the vinegar, salt, and baking soda. Beat for 2 minutes more. Scoop the batter into the prepared muffin tin. Bake for 18 to 20 minutes until a toothpick inserted into the center of one of the cupcakes comes out clean.

8. Remove from the oven and let the cupcakes cool in the pan for several minutes before removing them from the tin to a wire rack to cool completely.

TO MAKE THE FROSTING

1. In a large bowl, with a handheld electric mixer or in a stand mixer fitted with a whisk attachment, whip the butter and cream cheese for about 5 minutes until smooth.

2. With the mixer running on low speed, slowly add the powdered sugar, beating until thoroughly incorporated.

3. Add the vanilla and whip the frosting on medium-high speed until fluffy and light.

4. When the cupcakes are cool, pipe, spread, or scoop the frosting onto them and serve at room temperature.

Make-ahead tip: Make the cupcakes and frosting up to a day ahead. Refrigerate the cupcakes and frosting separately, covered with plastic wrap. Bring the frosting to room temperature before decorating the cupcakes.

TRES LECHES CAKE

※ Serves 12 ※

Tres leches is a sponge cake from Mexico. It's a basic white sheet cake doused with a mixture of three types of milk—*tres leches*—giving it a rich, custardy texture with tons of creamy flavor. A sweetened whipped cream topping finishes it off beautifully.

PREP TIME: 20 minutes

COOK TIME: 32 to 35 minutes

COOLING AND CHILLING TIME: 3 hours, 30 minutes

EQUIPMENT: 9-by-13-inch baking pan, electric mixer

Unsalted butter, for preparing
   the baking pan
All-purpose flour, for preparing
   the baking pan

FOR THE CAKE

5 eggs, separated
1 cup sugar, divided
⅓ cup whole milk
1 teaspoon vanilla extract
1 cup all-purpose flour
1½ teaspoons baking powder
¼ teaspoon salt

FOR THE FILLING

1 (14-ounce) can sweetened
   condensed milk
1 (12-ounce) can evaporated milk
½ cup heavy (whipping) cream

FOR THE WHIPPED CREAM TOPPING

1 pint heavy (whipping) cream
3 tablespoons powdered sugar
Ground cinnamon, for garnish

TO MAKE THE CAKE

1. Preheat the oven to 350°F.

2. Line a 9-by-13-inch pan with aluminum foil, and grease and flour the foil.

3. In a large bowl, using a handheld electric mixer or in a stand mixer on medium-high speed, beat together the egg yolks and ½ cup of sugar for about 4 minutes until the mixture becomes pale and doubles in volume.

4. Add the milk, vanilla, flour, baking powder, and salt. Turn the speed to low and beat until just combined.

5. In a medium bowl using a handheld electric mixer or a stand mixer on high speed, whip the egg whites until they hold soft peaks. Slowly add the remaining ½ cup of sugar and continue to whip on high speed until the mixture holds stiff peaks. Using a rubber spatula, gently fold the whipped egg whites into the cake batter. Transfer the batter to the prepared pan and bake for 32 to 35 minutes until springy to the touch and a toothpick inserted in the center comes out clean.

6. Remove from the oven and set the pan on a wire rack to cool for 30 minutes.

TO MAKE THE FILLING

1. In a medium bowl, stir together the sweetened condensed milk, evaporated milk, and cream until well combined.

2. Using a fork, poke holes all over the cake. Pour the filling over the top of the cake letting it seep into the holes.

3. Let the cake cool for at least 1 hour. Cover and refrigerate for at least 2 hours or overnight.

TO MAKE THE WHIPPED CREAM TOPPING

1. In a large bowl, using a handheld electric mixer or in a stand mixer on high speed, whip the heavy cream until soft peaks form.

2. Add the powdered sugar and beat until the mixture is well combined and reaches a thick, spreadable consistency. Spoon the whipped cream topping over the cake, smoothing it with a spatula.

3. Dust with cinnamon and serve immediately.

Make-ahead tip: The cake can be made and doused with the tres leches filling up to a day in advance. Refrigerate, covered. The whipped cream topping is best made just before decorating and serving.

BOURBON-CHOCOLATE BUNDT CAKE

➤— Serves 12 —➤

What I adore about this cake is that it looks pretty right
out of the pan. All it needs for adornment is a dusting of
powdered sugar. Since there's no need to bother with frosting
or elaborate decorations, it's an easy cake to whip up when
you need something that looks fancy, but doesn't require a
lot of time to fuss over it. Bourbon adds a grown-up kick.

PREP TIME: **15 minutes**
COOK TIME: **40 to 50 minutes**
COOLING TIME: **2 hours**
EQUIPMENT: **10-inch Bundt pan**

1 cup plus 3 tablespoons unsweetened
    cocoa powder, divided
1½ cups brewed coffee
½ cup bourbon whiskey
1 cup (2 sticks) unsalted butter,
    cut into 1-inch pieces, plus
    more for preparing the pan
2 cups sugar
2 cups all-purpose flour
1¼ teaspoons baking soda
½ teaspoon salt
2 eggs
1 teaspoon vanilla extract
Powdered sugar, for garnish

1. Preheat the oven to 325°F.

2. Grease a 10-inch Bundt pan and dust it
with 3 tablespoons of cocoa powder.

3. In a medium saucepan set over medium
heat, whisk the coffee, bourbon, butter, and
remaining 1 cup of cocoa powder until the
butter melts. Remove the pan from the heat
and whisk in the sugar until it dissolves. Pour
the mixture into a large bowl and let cool for
several minutes.

LEMON CHEESECAKE

— Serves 10 —

No-bake cheesecakes are the best for summer entertaining. There's no need to heat up your kitchen by turning on the oven, and they are, of course, decadently delicious. I love this tart-sweet lemon version set in a crunchy graham cracker crust.

PREP TIME: **15 minutes**
CHILLING TIME: **5 hours**
EQUIPMENT: **Electric mixer,**
9-inch springform pan

1½ cups finely ground graham
    cracker crumbs (from about
    9 graham crackers)
¼ cup packed brown sugar
6 tablespoons (¾ stick) unsalted
    butter, melted
1 cup heavy (whipping) cream
8 ounces cream cheese,
    at room temperature
½ cup lemon curd
⅓ cup powdered sugar
1 teaspoon vanilla extract

1. In a medium bowl, stir together the graham cracker crumbs, brown sugar, and butter until well combined. Press the mixture into the bottom and a bit up the sides of a 9-inch springform pan in an even layer. Refrigerate for 1 hour.

2. In a large bowl, using a handheld electric mixer or in a stand mixer, whip the cream until it holds stiff peaks.

3. In another large bowl, beat the cream cheese until it is creamy and smooth.

4. Beat the lemon curd, powdered sugar, and vanilla into the cream cheese.

5. Using a rubber spatula, gently fold in the whipped cream. Spoon the mixture into the prepared crust and use the rubber spatula to smooth the top. Refrigerate for at least 4 hours until completely set. Serve chilled.

Topping tip: Make a blueberry topping to spoon over your lemon cheesecake. Combine 3 cups fresh or frozen blueberries, 6 tablespoons sugar, 4 teaspoons cornstarch, and the juice of 1 lemon in a medium saucepan and cook for 8 to 10 minutes over medium heat until the blueberries break down and the sauce thickens. Chill completely before serving.

INDOOR
S'MORES CUPS

⊛— Makes 12 cups —⊛

Few combinations taste better than toasted marshmallows, chocolate, and graham crackers. After all, s'mores are the main reason people go camping, right? With this recipe, you can have all that fun without having to set up a tent or sleep outside. These are great for parties and are especially loved by children—of all ages.

PREP TIME: **15 minutes**

COOK TIME: **10 minutes**

EQUIPMENT: **12-cup muffin tin, foil cupcake liners**

Nonstick baking spray

10 graham crackers, crushed (about 2 cups)

½ cup (1 stick) plus 1 tablespoon unsalted butter, melted

½ cup sugar

¾ cup semisweet chocolate chips

1½ cups mini marshmallows

1. Preheat the oven to 350°F.

2. Line a 12-cup muffin tin with foil liners. Spray the inside of the liners with nonstick baking spray. You can skip the liners if you like and just spray the tin, but the s'mores may crumble a bit when removed from the pan.

3. In a medium bowl, stir together the graham cracker crumbs, butter, and sugar until thoroughly combined. Put about 2 tablespoons of the mixture into each muffin cup and press it firmly into the bottom of the cup. Bake for 5 minutes.

4. Remove the muffin tin from the oven and let cool. Leave the oven on.

5. Divide half the chocolate chips and half the marshmallows evenly among the cups. Top the marshmallows with a second layer of graham cracker crumbs, about 1½ to 2 table-spoons of crumbs in each cup. Press down firmly to pack the crumb mixture. Return to the oven and bake for 4 minutes.

6. Remove the muffin tin from the oven and turn on the broiler. Add the remaining chocolate chips and marshmallows to the cups,

dividing equally, and put the pan under the broiler for 2 to 3 minutes until the marshmallows are toasted and golden brown.

7. Remove from the oven and let the cups cool in the pan for 15 minutes before removing them from the tin to a wire rack to cool completely.

Technique tip: Use a small juice glass or something similar to press the crumbs firmly into the bottom of the muffin cups.

Left: Nectarine Galette (page 133)

STRAWBERRY CREAM PIE

❦— Serves 6 —❦

When strawberry season rolls around, there is nothing better than combining those sweet berries with a creamy no-bake pie filling set in a shortbread-cookie-crumb crust. Mascarpone is a soft, mild Italian cheese made with cream, giving it a high fat content and a luxurious mouthfeel. If you can't find it, substitute a good full-fat ricotta cheese.

PREP TIME: 20 minutes

CHILLING AND FREEZING TIME: 5 hours

EQUIPMENT: 9-inch pie dish

FOR THE CRUST

2¾ cups (about 11 ounces) crushed shortbread cookie crumbs

1 tablespoon sugar

6 tablespoons (¾ stick) unsalted butter, melted

FOR THE FILLING

1½ cups sliced fresh strawberries

2 tablespoons sugar

¾ cup mascarpone cheese, at room temperature

¾ cup plain Greek yogurt, at room temperature

¼ cup plus 2 tablespoons powdered sugar

CONTINUED →

NO-BAKE STRAWBERRY CREAM PIE
continued

TO MAKE THE CRUST

In a medium bowl, stir together the cookie crumbs, sugar, and butter until thoroughly combined and beginning to clump. Press the mixture into the bottom and up the sides of a 9-inch pie dish, pressing firmly. Freeze for 1 hour.

TO MAKE THE FILLING

1. When the crust is frozen, put the strawberries in a medium bowl and toss with the sugar. Let the strawberries sit to macerate for 15 minutes.

2. While the strawberries sit, in a medium bowl, stir together the mascarpone, yogurt, and powdered sugar to mix well. Spread half the mascarpone-yogurt mixture in an even layer on top of the crust.

3. Layer half the strawberries on top and cover them with the remaining mascarpone-yogurt mixture. Arrange the remaining strawberries on top.

4. Refrigerate for at least 4 hours before slicing into wedges and serving.

Technique tip: If you want to shorten the waiting time, bake the cookie-crumb crust in a 350°F oven for about 8 minutes instead of freezing it for 1 hour.

MAPLE SYRUP CREAM PIE

⸙ Serves 8 ⸙

Maple syrup has one of the most heavenly flavors, and it's not just for covering pancakes and French toast. This delicious no-bake pie delivers intense maple flavor in a creamy, smooth filling. It's a Canadian version of Sweet and Creamy Sugar Cream Pie (page 124) and is traditionally made to celebrate the springtime syrup-making season.

PREP TIME: **10 minutes**
CHILLING TIME: **4 hours**
EQUIPMENT: **9-inch pie dish, medium saucepan**

1½ cups maple syrup (see tip)
1 cup heavy (whipping) cream
¼ cup cornstarch mixed with
    ¼ cup cold water
1 (9-inch) piecrust (prebaked, homemade, or store-bought and baked according to the package directions)

1. In a medium saucepan set over medium-high heat, whisk the maple syrup and cream. Bring to a simmer.

2. Whisking constantly, add the cornstarch mixture. Still whisking constantly, bring the mixture to a boil and cook for about 2 minutes, lowering the heat if necessary to keep it from burning, until the mixture thickens. Pour the maple-cream mixture into the piecrust and refrigerate for at least 4 hours until set. Serve chilled.

Ingredient tip: When choosing maple syrup, remember that the darker the color, the more intense the maple flavor will be. Since maple syrup is the star of this show, I like to use a dark amber or grade B syrup for this pie.

FRENCH SILK PIE

WITH SHORTBREAD CRUST

⊰–– Serves 8 ––⊱

You won't believe how easy it is to make this rich, creamy chocolate cream pie. The shortbread-cookie-crumb crust doesn't even need to be baked and it adds a buttery, crumbly, sweet base layer that may be even better than a regular piecrust. Make this for any special occasion. Like, you know, an average Tuesday night dinner.

PREP TIME: **20 minutes**

CHILLING TIME: **3 hours**

EQUIPMENT: **9-inch pie dish, electric mixer**

FOR THE CRUST

2 ¾ cups (about 11 ounces) crushed shortbread cookie crumbs

1 tablespoon sugar

6 tablespoons (¾ stick) unsalted butter, melted

FOR THE FILLING

⅔ cup sugar

2 eggs

2 ounces unsweetened baking chocolate, chopped

⅓ cup unsalted butter, left at room temperature for 15 to 20 minutes before using

1½ cups heavy (whipping) cream

¼ cup powdered sugar

Chocolate shavings, for garnish

TO MAKE THE CRUST

In large bowl, stir together the cookie crumbs, sugar, and butter until well combined. Press the mixture into the bottom and up the sides of 9-inch pie dish. Refrigerate for 1 hour before proceeding with the recipe.

TO MAKE THE FILLING

1. In a small saucepan, whisk the sugar and eggs until well mixed. Place the pan over medium heat and cook for about 4 minutes until the mixture is thick enough to coat the back of a spoon. Remove the pan from the heat and stir in the chocolate, stirring until it is completely melted and the mixture is smooth. Let cool for a few minutes.

2. Mix in the butter, stirring until it is fully incorporated. Transfer to a large bowl and refrigerate the mixture while you make the whipped cream.

3. In another large bowl, using a handheld electric mixer or a stand mixer, whip the cream until it holds soft peaks.

4. Add the powdered sugar and continue to whip until it holds stiff peaks. Add half the whipped cream to the cooled chocolate mixture and gently fold it in with a rubber spatula. Pour the chocolate mixture into the prepared crust.

5. Dollop the remaining whipped cream on top and garnish with chocolate shavings. Refrigerate for at least 2 hours before serving.

Ingredient tip: The eggs in this recipe aren't fully cooked. If you are concerned about eating raw or undercooked eggs, use pasteurized eggs.

NO-BAKE
MOCHA MUD PIE

⊰⊱ Serves 8 ⊰⊱

This mud pie strays from the traditional pudding-filled concoction
you may be used to, but it fulfills any chocoholic's fantasy, and
then some. It's a chocolate-cookie-crumb crust filled with a rich,
espresso-flavored, chocolatey cream cheese mixture, all topped with
sweetened whipped cream, chocolate shavings, and hot fudge sauce.

PREP TIME: **20 minutes**

CHILLING TIME: **4 hours, 30 minutes**

EQUIPMENT: **9-inch pie dish,
electric mixer**

1 tablespoon instant espresso powder

1½ cups crushed chocolate wafer
    cookies (I prefer Nabisco
    Famous Chocolate Wafers)

6 tablespoons (¾ stick) unsalted
    butter, melted

3 ounces semisweet
    chocolate, chopped

2 cups heavy (whipping) cream

¾ cup powdered sugar, divided

1 (8-ounce) package cream cheese,
    at room temperature

½ teaspoon vanilla extract

Chocolate shavings, for garnish

1 cup hot fudge sauce

1. In a measuring cup, mix the espresso
powder into ¼ cup water. Set aside to let
the espresso powder dissolve.

2. In a medium bowl, stir together the
chocolate wafer crumbs and butter until
well combined. Press the mixture firmly into
a 9-inch pie dish. Refrigerate for 30 minutes.

3. Meanwhile, in a small microwave-safe
bowl, microwave the chocolate at 50 percent power, in 30-second intervals, stirring
in between, until melted and smooth.

4. In a large bowl, with a handheld electric
mixer or in a stand mixer, whip the heavy
cream until it holds soft peaks. Add ½ cup
of powdered sugar along with the vanilla.
Whip until the mixture holds stiff peaks.

5. In another large bowl, beat together the cream cheese and remaining ¼ cup of powdered sugar until thoroughly combined.

6. Add the dissolved espresso powder and stir to incorporate completely.

7. Add the melted chocolate to the cream cheese mixture and mix to combine.

8. Gently fold 2 cups of whipped cream mixture into the cream cheese-and-chocolate mixture. Transfer to the prepared crust and smooth the top with a rubber spatula.

9. Spread the remaining whipped cream on top and garnish with chocolate shavings. Refrigerate the pie for at least 4 hours before serving.

10. Serve chilled with hot fudge sauce drizzled over the top.

Make-ahead tip: This pie is even better the day after it's made, so go ahead and make it in advance. Keep it covered in the refrigerator until ready to serve.

SUGAR CREAM PIE

⊰⊱— Serves 8 —⊰⊱

This scrumptious dessert is exactly what it sounds like, a pie filled with a sweet cream custard. It is delightfully simple and absolutely irresistible. The rich creamy filling is the star of this dessert, so I recommend saving the time and effort and using a good-quality store-bought piecrust.

PREP TIME: **10 minutes**
COOK TIME: **40 minutes**
COOLING TIME: **1 hour**
EQUIPMENT: **9-inch pie dish**

½ cup granulated sugar
½ cup packed dark brown sugar
2 tablespoons all-purpose flour
2 cups heavy (whipping) cream
½ teaspoon vanilla extract
1 (9-inch) piecrust (prebaked, homemade, or store-bought and baked according to the package directions)
Powdered sugar, for dusting

1. Preheat the oven to 400°F.

2. In a medium bowl, whisk the granulated sugar, brown sugar, and flour, breaking up any clumps.

3. In another medium bowl, stir together the cream and vanilla.

4. While whisking constantly, add the cream to the sugar mixture in a slow, steady stream. Whisk until the mixture is well combined and smooth. Pour the filling into the par-baked crust and bake the pie for about 40 minutes until the filling is set around the edges.

5. Remove the pie from the oven and set it on a wire rack to cool completely, at least 1 hour.

6. Sprinkle powdered sugar over the top of the pie, slice it into wedges, and serve at room temperature.

Technique tip: If the pie is getting too dark too fast, loosely tent it with aluminum foil for the last 10 minutes of baking.

COCONUT CUSTARD PIE

⁕ Serves 8 ⁕

This pie is similar to the magic pudding cakes in chapter 3 (see Magic Lemon Pudding Cake, page 44, and Chocolate Brownie Pudding Cake, page 46) because it bakes into two distinct layers—crust and custardy filling. You get the creamy, delicious coconut flavor of a coconut cream pie, but with far less effort.

PREP TIME: **5 minutes**

COOK TIME: **50 minutes to 1 hour**

COOLING AND CHILLING TIME: **5 hours**

EQUIPMENT: **9-inch pie dish**

6 tablespoons (¾ stick) unsalted butter, at room temperature, plus more for preparing the pie dish

½ cup all-purpose flour, plus more for preparing the pie dish

1 (14-ounce) can sweetened condensed milk

1 (13-ounce) can coconut milk

4 eggs

1½ cups sweetened, flaked coconut, divided

1 teaspoon vanilla extract

¼ teaspoon salt

1. Preheat the oven to 350°F.

2. Grease a 9-inch pie dish with butter and dust it with flour.

3. In a large bowl, using an electric mixer or a whisk, or in a blender, combine the sweetened condensed milk, coconut milk, eggs, 1 cup of shredded coconut, butter, flour, vanilla, and salt. Beat until smooth. Pour the mixture into the prepared pie dish and bake for 50 minutes to 1 hour until the center is mostly set.

4. Remove from the oven and set the pie on a wire rack to cool to room temperature, about 1 hour. Transfer to the refrigerator and chill for at least 4 hours until completely set.

5. Just before serving, sprinkle the remaining coconut over the top. Cut into wedges and serve chilled.

Technique tip: Toasting the coconut makes its flavor deeper and more complex. I like to toast the coconut that I'm putting on top of this pie because it not only tastes great, but looks pretty, too. Spread it on a baking sheet and toast in a 325°F oven for about 5 minutes, stirring occasionally, until golden brown.

DARK CHOCOLATE PECAN PIE

⚜— Serves 10 —⚜

The classic Southern pecan pie gets even better when you add dark chocolate and a splash of bourbon to the filling. Using a store-bought piecrust makes it easy to pull together, although you can make your own if you are into that sort of thing.

PREP TIME: **20 minutes**
COOK TIME: **30 to 40 minutes**
COOLING TIME: **2 hours**
EQUIPMENT: **9-inch pie dish, large rimmed baking sheet, small saucepan**

1½ cups pecan halves
6 tablespoons (¾ stick) unsalted butter
2 ounces bittersweet chocolate, chopped
¾ cup dark corn syrup
4 eggs
½ cup packed light brown sugar
1 tablespoon unsweetened cocoa powder
2 tablespoons bourbon
¼ teaspoon salt
1 (9-inch) piecrust (prebaked, homemade, or store-bought and baked according to the package directions)

1. Preheat the oven to 350°F.

2. Spread the pecans in a single layer on a large rimmed baking sheet and bake for 8 to 10 minutes.

3. Remove from the oven and let cool. Leave the oven on.

4. While the nuts cool, in a small saucepan set over low heat, combine the butter and chocolate. Cook, stirring constantly, until both are melted and the mixture is smooth. Remove from the heat and transfer the mixture to a large bowl. Let cool.

5. Add the corn syrup, eggs, brown sugar, cocoa powder, bourbon, and salt to the cooled chocolate mixture and whisk well to combine. Pour the filling into the crust and arrange the pecans in a single layer on top of the filling. Bake for 30 to 40 minutes, until the filling is just barely set.

6. Remove from the oven and place the pie on a wire rack to cool completely, at least 2 hours, before serving.

Ingredient tip: If you are using a store-bought piecrust, follow the instructions on the package for prebaking it. Bake it in a 9-inch pie dish, or if you bought a pre-formed crust, leave it in the disposable aluminum foil baking dish it came in.

GINGER AND SPICE PUMPKIN PIE

⋙— Serves 8 —⋘

Fresh ginger along with cinnamon and cloves give a flavorful kick
to this classic pie filling. By using canned pumpkin purée and a
store-bought piecrust, this festive dessert can be pulled together
in a matter of minutes. Serve it for Thanksgiving, or any special
holiday meal, with lots of sweetened whipped cream on top.

PREP TIME: **10 minutes**

COOK TIME: **40 to 50 minutes**

EQUIPMENT: **9-inch pie dish**

1 uncooked 9-inch piecrust
(homemade or store-bought)
1 (15-ounce) can pumpkin purée
¾ cup sugar
¾ cup heavy (whipping) cream
2 eggs
1 tablespoon grated fresh ginger
½ teaspoon ground cinnamon
¼ teaspoon salt
Pinch ground cloves
Whipped cream, for serving

1. Preheat the oven to 350°F.

2. Fit the piecrust into a 9-inch pie dish.

3. In a large bowl, whisk the pumpkin purée,
sugar, cream, eggs, ginger, cinnamon,
salt, and cloves until thoroughly combined. Spoon the mixture into the piecrust,
smoothing the top with a rubber spatula.
Bake for 40 to 50 minutes until just set in
the center.

4. Remove from the oven and set the pie
on a wire rack to cool to room temperature.
Serve warm, dolloped with whipped cream.

Make-ahead tip: This pie keeps well in the
refrigerator, covered, for up to 2 days. Bring it
to room temperature before serving.

TARTE TATIN

Whether it's the French name, the luscious golden caramel, or the flaky puff pastry, this dish never fails to impress. The good news is it is a no-fuss prep. The apple slices become meltingly tender as they cook in the rich caramel beneath a flaky pastry shell. Flip the whole thing over after baking for a stunning caramel-apple tart.

PREP TIME: **15 minutes**

COOK TIME: **50 minutes**

EQUIPMENT: **small saucepan, 9-inch round cake pan**

All-purpose flour, for dusting
    the work surface
1 sheet (about 8 ounces) puff pastry
4 tablespoons salted butter
4 tablespoons sugar
6 Golden Delicious apples, peeled,
    cored, and cut into wedges
Crème fraîche or vanilla ice cream,
    for serving

1. Preheat the oven to 425°F.

2. On a lightly floured work surface, roll out the pastry sheet and trim it to fit a 9-inch round cake pan. Wrap the dough in plastic wrap and refrigerate until ready to use.

3. In a small saucepan set over medium heat, melt the butter.

4. Add the sugar, sprinkling it evenly over the butter. Cook for about 5 minutes, stirring occasionally, until the mixture is golden brown. Remove the pan from the heat and pour the caramel into the cake pan, spreading it evenly over the bottom.

CONTINUED →

5. Arrange the apples in a single layer on top of the caramel. Bake for 30 minutes.

6. Remove the pan from the oven (leaving the oven on) and place the puff pastry on top of the apples. Use a sharp knife to cut 4 steam vents in the crust. Return to the oven and bake for about 20 minutes more until the pastry is golden brown.

7. Remove the pan from the oven and carefully invert the tart onto a wire rack. You may want to place a baking sheet underneath the rack to catch any messy caramel drips.

8. Cut into wedges and serve warm or at room temperature, topped with crème fraiche or vanilla ice cream.

Ingredient tip: Store-bought puff pastry is one of those shortcuts I find completely worthwhile, since making your own requires a great deal of effort and high-quality premade versions are widely available. For the best flavor, check the ingredients and buy one that uses only butter for fat. Avoid puff pastry brands made with shortening or other fats.

FRESH FRUIT TARTLETS
WITH PASTRY CREAM

⸺ Makes 12 tartlets ⸺

Once again, a store-bought piecrust saves the day, helping these tartlets come together with very little hands-on time. I love these topped with mixed berries or sliced stone fruits such as peaches, nectarines, or pears. Their small size and colorful topping possibilities make them a great dessert for any celebratory event.

PREP TIME: **20 minutes**
COOK TIME: **18 to 22 minutes**
CHILLING TIME: **2 hours**
EQUIPMENT: **12-cup muffin tin,**
3½-inch round cookie cutter

All-purpose flour, for dusting the
   work surface
1 uncooked 9-inch piecrust
   (homemade or store-bought)
4 egg yolks
½ cup sugar
¼ cup cornstarch
Pinch salt
2 cups low-fat or whole milk
1½ teaspoons vanilla extract
Fresh fruit, for topping the tartlets
   (sliced peaches, nectarines,
   strawberries, raspberries,
   blueberries, or other fruit
   as desired)

1. Preheat the oven to 400°F.

2. On a lightly floured work surface, Roll out the piecrust to an even thickness of about ⅛ inch. Using a 3½-inch round cookie cutter, cut out 12 dough circles. Fit the dough circles into the cups of a muffin tin, pressing them in to form little dough cups. Bake for 11 to 13 minutes until they are lightly golden brown. Transfer the cups to a wire rack to cool completely.

3. While the cups cool, make the filling. In a medium bowl, whisk the egg yolks until smooth.

CONTINUED →

FRESH FRUIT TARTLETS WITH PASTRY CREAM

continued

4. In a saucepan set over medium heat, combine the sugar, cornstarch, and salt. Whisking continuously, add the milk in a slow, steady stream. Cook for about 5 minutes, whisking, until the mixture bubbles and thickens.

5. While whisking constantly, ladle about ⅓ of the milk mixture into the egg yolks. Transfer the egg yolk mixture to the saucepan, still whisking constantly, and bring to a boil. Cook for 2 to 4 minutes, whisking, until the mixture is very thick. Remove the saucepan from the heat and

stir in the vanilla. Transfer the pastry cream to a bowl, cover with plastic wrap, and refrigerate for 2 hours.

6. Spoon, pipe, or scoop the pastry cream into the tart shells. Top with fresh fruit and serve immediately.

Technique tip: For especially pretty tartlets, use a scalloped cookie cutter. The edges will be turned up when you press the dough into the muffin tin, giving your tartlets a pretty finished edge.

NECTARINE GALETTE

Serves 6

This rustic galette is so easy, yet like other desserts in this book, looks like you labored over it for hours. If you use a store-bought piecrust (as you can tell, I swear by these), you'll be able to put together this fancy-looking tart and get it in the oven in less than 10 minutes.

PREP TIME: **10 minutes**
COOK TIME: **12 to 15 minutes**
EQUIPMENT: **Baking sheet, pastry brush**

1 uncooked 9-inch piecrust
   (homemade or store-bought)
4 to 5 ripe nectarines, cut into wedges
3 tablespoons sugar, divided
1 tablespoon cornstarch
1 egg, beaten

1. Preheat the oven to 425°F.

2. Line a baking sheet with parchment paper and lay the piecrust out on the prepared sheet.

3. In a medium bowl, toss together the nectarine slices, 2 tablespoons of sugar, and the cornstarch. Transfer the mixture to a colander over the sink and let it drain for a few minutes. Pour the fruit onto the piecrust, mounding it in the center and leaving a 2-inch border of crust all the way around the fruit.

4. Fold the uncovered sides of the crust up over the edges of the fruit and fold into pleats to make a rustic circle.

5. Brush the beaten egg over the crust and sprinkle the remaining tablespoon of sugar over the crust. Bake for 12 to 15 minutes until the crust is golden brown.

6. Remove from the oven and let cool. Serve warm or at room temperature.

Substitution tip: Use just about any fruit in place of the nectarines. Peaches, plums, or pitted and halved cherries all lead to a spectacular dessert.

CANNOLI CREAM-FILLED MINI TARTLETS

— Makes 24 mini tartlets —

Cannoli—delicate fried tubes of pastry dough filled with a sweetened ricotta cream often studded with dried fruit or bits of chocolate—are a rare and special treat, as making them is laborious. My family adores them, but we have them only when we happen to be close to our favorite Italian bakery—which is 3,000 miles away from where we live! These sweet tartlets filled with cannoli cream are a fine substitute. They have all the irresistible flavor of real Italian bakery cannoli, but they're a breeze to make.

PREP TIME: **20 minutes**

COOK TIME: **11 to 13 minutes**

CHILLING TIME: **30 minutes**

EQUIPMENT: **24-cup mini muffin tin, 2½-inch round cookie cutter**

All-purpose flour, for dusting the work surface

1 uncooked 9-inch piecrust (homemade or store-bought)

12 ounces whole-milk ricotta cheese, drained

8 ounces mascarpone cheese

½ cup plus 2 tablespoons powdered sugar, plus more for dusting

½ cup mini semisweet chocolate chips

1. Preheat the oven to 400°F.

2. On a lightly floured surface, roll out the piecrust to an even thickness of about ⅛ inch.

3. Using a 2½-inch round cookie cutter, cut out 24 dough circles. Fit the dough circles into the cups of a mini muffin tin, pressing them in to form little dough cups. Bake for 11 to 13 minutes until lightly golden brown. Transfer the cups to a wire rack to cool completely.

4. While the cups cool, make the filling. In a large bowl, with a rubber spatula, stir together the ricotta and mascarpone cheeses until well combined and smooth.

5. Add the powdered sugar and stir to incorporate well.

6. Stir in the chocolate chips and mix well. Cover and refrigerate for at least 30 minutes.

7. When ready to fill the cups, transfer the filling to a piping bag or a resealable plastic bag with the tip cut off one bottom corner. Pipe the filling into the pastry cups.

8. Dust with powdered sugar and serve. Cover and refrigerate any leftovers for up to 3 days.

Technique tip: Instead of piping the filling into the cups, use a large cookie scoop to fill them.

NO-BAKE
CHOCOLATE-PEANUT BUTTER TART

⊰⊱ Serves 6 ⊰⊱

A simple graham cracker crust provides a crunchy, sweet
base for velvety layers of chocolate ganache and peanut
butter cream. With a classic flavor combination and a smooth,
refined filling, this no-bake tart is a surefire winner. Serve
it topped with dollops of whipped cream if desired.

PREP TIME: 20 minutes
CHILLING TIME: 2 hours
EQUIPMENT: 9-inch round tart
or cake pan

FOR THE CRUST
10 graham crackers, crushed
(about 2 cups)
6 tablespoons (¾ stick) unsalted
butter, melted

FOR THE FILLING
3 ounces milk chocolate, chopped,
plus more to make chocolate curls
for garnish
1¼ cups heavy (whipping)
cream, divided
¾ cup creamy peanut butter
4 ounces cream cheese,
at room temperature
⅓ cup sweetened condensed milk

TO MAKE THE CRUST

In a medium bowl, stir together the graham cracker crumbs and butter until thoroughly combined. Press the mixture into the bottom and up the sides of a 9-inch round tart or cake pan. Refrigerate the crust while you prepare the filling.

TO MAKE THE FILLING

1. In a medium microwave-safe bowl, combine the chocolate and ½ cup of cream. Microwave at 50 percent power, in 30-second intervals, stirring in between, until the chocolate is completely melted and the mixture is smooth. Let cool, whisking occasionally. Once cool and thick, spread the chocolate ganache into the bottom of the prepared crust in an even layer. Refrigerate the crust again until ready to add the peanut butter filling.

2. In a medium bowl, stir together the peanut butter, cream cheese, and sweetened condensed milk.

3. In a large bowl, using a handheld electric mixer or in a stand mixer fitted with the whisk attachment, whip the remaining ¾ cup of cream until it holds soft peaks. Gently fold the whipped cream into the peanut butter mixture. Spread the mixture in the crust on top of the chocolate layer, smoothing the top with a rubber spatula. Return the filled tart to the refrigerator for at least 2 hours until set.

4. Garnish the chilled tart with chocolate curls, slice into wedges, and serve.

Make-ahead tip: This tart can be made up to 2 days ahead. Refrigerate, covered, until ready to serve.

CRUSTLESS
PEAR CUSTARD TART

— Serves 6 —

This recipe has only six ingredients and takes only five minutes to put together. You'll wonder how it can possibly be so good with such little effort. Here we bake tender pears in a sweet, custardy batter. The result is sublime. Instead of making one big tart, you can make six individual ones if you have mini tart tins.

PREP TIME: **5 minutes**
COOK TIME: **20 to 30 minutes**
EQUIPMENT: **9-inch round cake pan**

¾ cup (1½ sticks) unsalted butter, plus more for preparing the cake pan
⅓ cup all-purpose flour
1½ cups powdered sugar, plus more for dusting
1 cup almond meal
3 eggs, beaten
3 pears, cored and cut into wedges

1. Preheat the oven to 400°F.

2. Lightly grease a 9-inch round cake pan.

3. In a small saucepan set over medium heat, melt the butter and cook for about 3 minutes until it just turns golden brown. Remove from the heat and let cool.

4. Meanwhile, in a medium bowl, stir together the flour, powdered sugar, and almond meal.

5. Add the melted butter and the eggs and stir to combine thoroughly. Pour the batter into the prepared pan and arrange the pear wedges on top. Bake for 15 minutes, lower the heat to 350°F, then bake for 5 to 10 minutes more, until just golden brown.

6. Dust with powdered sugar, slice into wedges, and serve warm or at room temperature.

Topping tip: A dollop of lightly sweetened whipped cream, crème fraîche, or vanilla ice cream finishes this dessert nicely.

DOUBLE CHOCOLATE GANACHE TART

—⟡— Serves 6 —⟡—

A rich chocolate-ganache-filled chocolate-cookie-crumb crust is a thing of beauty. Topped with fluffy whipped cream and sweet, ruby-red raspberries, it provides a photo-worthy end to any meal.

PREP TIME: **15 minutes**
COOK TIME: **20 minutes**
CHILLING TIME: **1 hour**
EQUIPMENT: **9-inch tart pan** with a removable bottom

32 chocolate wafer cookies (about 8 ounces), crushed into fine crumbs (I prefer Nabisco Famous Chocolate Wafers)
2 tablespoons sugar
½ teaspoon salt
6 tablespoons (¾ stick) unsalted butter, melted
12 ounces semisweet chocolate, chopped
1¼ cups heavy (whipping) cream
Lightly sweetened whipped cream, for serving
1½ cups fresh raspberries

1. Preheat the oven to 350°F.

2. In a medium bowl, stir together the cookie crumbs, sugar, and salt.

3. Stir in the melted butter and mix until well combined. Press the cookie-crumb mixture into the bottom and up the sides of a 9-inch tart pan with a removable bottom. Bake for 20 minutes.

4. Remove from the oven and let cool.

5. In a medium microwave-safe bowl, combine the chocolate and cream. Microwave at 50 percent power, in 30-second intervals, stirring in between, until the chocolate is completely melted and the mixture is smooth. Pour the chocolate mixture into the prepared crust. Refrigerate for at least 1 hour until set.

6. Serve chilled, cut into wedges, and garnished with whipped cream and raspberries

Make-ahead tip: This tart stores well, so it's a great choice for a make-ahead dessert. Refrigerate it for up to 1 week or freeze it for up to 1 month. If you freeze it, thaw it in the refrigerator overnight before serving.

Chapter Seven

HOMEMADE CANDIES,
CHOCOLATES & FUDGE

Left: Dark Chocolate, Cherry, and Hazelnut Bark (page 154)

MELT-IN-YOUR-MOUTH
BUTTERMINTS

⊰⊱ Makes about 1 pound ⊰⊱

These are often called wedding mints as they are traditionally served alongside the cake at wedding receptions. Regardless, they make great treats for any occasion. You will be surprised at how easy—and fun—these candies are to make. They are little pillows of airy, melt-in-your-mouth, minty, buttery, sweet candy. Eating them is only a little more fun than making them.

PREP TIME: **15 minutes**

DRYING TIME: **12 hours**

EQUIPMENT: **Baking sheet, electric mixer**

½ cup (1 stick) unsalted butter, removed from the refrigerator about 15 minutes before using

2 tablespoons heavy (whipping) cream

1 teaspoon peppermint extract

Pinch salt

3 ¾ cups powdered sugar, divided, plus more for dusting your hands

1. Line a large baking sheet with parchment paper.

2. In a large bowl, using an electric mixer or in a stand mixer fitted with a whisk attachment set on high speed, beat the butter until it is fluffy and light. With a rubber spatula, scrape down the sides of the bowl.

3. Add the cream, peppermint extract, and salt. Beat to combine thoroughly.

4. Add 1½ cups of powdered sugar and beat on low speed until combined. Add another 1½ cups of powdered sugar and mix until thoroughly incorporated. Add the remaining ¾ cup of powdered sugar and beat until incorporated. Raise the mixer speed to high and beat for about 4 minutes until the mixture becomes very airy and light.

5. Coat your hands lightly with powdered sugar and pick up the dough ball, rolling it between your hands to make a rope about as thick as your thumb. Using a sharp knife, cut the rope into ¾-inch-long pieces.

Arrange the mints on the prepared sheet in a single layer. Leave the baking sheet out, uncovered, at room temperature for about 12 hours until the candies are dry. Serve immediately or refrigerate in an airtight container for up to 1 week.

Technique tip: These turn out a pretty, if understated, off-white color. If you'd like something more colorful, add a few drops of food coloring to the dough. You could also split the dough into 2 or 3 segments and use a different color for each.

HOMEMADE CARAMELS

⊷— Makes 64 (1-inch) caramels —⊶

Rich, creamy, buttery, sweet caramels are like little bites of delight. I always thought they were too complicated to make— that is, until I discovered this recipe. It's quick, uncomplicated, and doesn't require any special equipment. The best part: It only uses six ingredients. Now I make them every chance I get.

PREP TIME: **10 minutes**
COOK TIME: **10 minutes**
COOLING TIME: **1 to 2 hours**
EQUIPMENT: **8-inch square baking pan**

¾ cup (1½ sticks) unsalted butter
½ cup sugar
3 tablespoons light corn syrup
1 (14-ounce) can sweetened
   condensed milk
¼ teaspoon salt
½ teaspoon vanilla extract

1. Line an 8-inch square baking pan with aluminum foil.

2. In a medium saucepan set over medium heat, stir together the butter and sugar. When the butter is completely melted, add the corn syrup, sweetened condensed milk, and salt. Stir to combine.

3. Raise the heat to medium-high and bring the mixture to a boil. Lower the heat and let the mixture cook for about 10 minutes (it should be bubbling vigorously), stirring constantly, until it turns a deep golden brown. At this point, the caramel should be pulling away from the sides of the pan as you stir. Remove the pan from the heat and immediately stir in the vanilla.

4. Transfer the caramel to the prepared baking pan and let cool completely, 1 to 2 hours.

5. Cut the cooled caramel into squares and serve immediately, or wrap in wax paper and store at room temperature for up to 2 weeks.

Topping tip: Sprinkle with a flaky sea salt, such as fleur de sel, after pouring the caramel into the pan.

HONEYCOMB CANDY

CRISPY-CRUNCHY

—❈— Serves 8 —❈—

I can't get enough of the way this airy, light candy crunches between my teeth. I love the fancy look of it as it puffs up with millions of tiny air bubbles when it cools. It seems like it would be difficult to make something with such a magical texture, but all it takes is a little bit of baking soda sprinkled in at just the right moment. I like to add this to a gift box of holiday candies or serve it on a cookie tray.

PREP TIME: **5 minutes**

COOK TIME: **10 minutes**

COOLING TIME: **30 minutes**

EQUIPMENT: **Medium saucepan, baking sheet**

¼ cup plus 1 tablespoon sugar

¼ cup honey

Pinch salt

1½ teaspoons baking soda

1. Line a baking sheet with parchment paper.

2. In a medium saucepan set over medium-high heat, stir together the sugar, honey, and salt. Bring to a boil. Cook for about 10 minutes, stirring frequently, until the mixture turns deep golden brown. Remove the pan from the heat and quickly stir in the baking soda. Be careful as the mixture will bubble and foam up dramatically. Stir until the baking soda dissolves completely.

3. Pour the mixture onto the prepared sheet and let cool to room temperature, about 30 minutes. When cool, it will be fully set.

4. Break into pieces to serve.

Make-ahead tip: Make the honeycomb ahead and store it in an airtight container at room temperature for up to 1 week.

QUICK AND EASY
PEANUT BRITTLE

— Serves 10 —

Peanut brittle is surprisingly effortless to make on the stove top, but use the microwave and it gets *even easier*. If you like salty-sweet treats, add more salt or a sprinkle of flaky sea salt, such as fleur de sel, on top after the brittle cools.

PREP TIME: **20 minutes**
COOLING TIME: **1 to 2 hours**
EQUIPMENT: **Baking sheet**

Nonstick baking spray
1 cup sugar
½ cup light corn syrup
1 cup unsalted peanuts
¼ teaspoon salt
1 tablespoon unsalted butter
1 teaspoon vanilla extract
1 teaspoon baking soda

1. Spray a baking sheet with nonstick baking spray.

2. In a large microwave-safe bowl, whisk the sugar and corn syrup. Microwave at full power for 4 minutes.

3. Stir in the peanuts and salt to combine. Microwave again at full power for 3½ minutes.

4. Stir in the butter and vanilla until the butter melts completely. Return to the microwave and microwave at full power for 1½ minutes more.

5. Immediately stir in the baking soda. The mixture will foam up. Transfer the mixture to the prepared sheet, and with a rubber spatula, gently spread it into an even layer.

6. Let cool completely for 1 to 2 hours. To serve, break the brittle into pieces.

Variation tip: Use any nuts you like in place of the peanuts. Almonds, cashews, or pecans are all great substitutes.

MIMOSA JELLY CANDIES

⊰— Makes 64 (1-inch) candies —⊱

These sparkling jelly candies are a fun treat for any celebration where you might have champagne or mimosas: a wedding, wedding shower, anniversary party, or milestone birthday. And they're alcohol free, so they're kid friendly. They require only a few ingredients, some of which you likely have in your kitchen. You can find flavoring oils at baking and candy-making supply shops, craft shops that carry baking supplies (such as Michaels and Jo-Ann Fabrics), or online. You can substitute flavor extracts, too, but will need to increase the amount, as oils are stronger than extracts (see tip on page 152).

PREP TIME: **5 minutes**

COOK TIME: **30 minutes**

CHILLING AND SETTING TIME:

28 to 52 hours

EQUIPMENT: **8-inch square baking pan**

Nonstick baking spray

3 tablespoons unflavored gelatin
  (about 4 envelopes)

3 cups sugar, plus more for
  coating the candies

¼ to ½ teaspoon orange flavoring oil

¼ to ½ teaspoon champagne
  flavoring oil

Orange food coloring, for
  coloring the candies

1. Line an 8-inch square baking pan with plastic wrap (let the plastic wrap hang over the sides of the pan for easy removal) and spray with nonstick baking spray.

2. Put ¾ cup cold water into a medium saucepan, sprinkle the gelatin evenly over the top, and let sit for 5 minutes.

3. In another pot or a kettle, bring 1 cup plus 2 tablespoons water to a boil. Once the gelatin has been sitting in the cold water for 5 minutes, add the boiling water to the saucepan. Stir the mixture until the gelatin dissolves completely.

4. Add the sugar and stir to combine. Place the saucepan over medium-high heat and bring the mixture to a boil. Lower the heat to medium and simmer for 25 minutes, stirring constantly. Remove the pan from the heat.

5. Stir in the orange and champagne flavoring oils to taste. Add orange food coloring to your desired color. Pour the hot mixture into the prepared pan. Cover with plastic wrap and refrigerate for at least 4 hours until completely set.

6. Lift the set jelly from the pan using the plastic wrap. Peel off the plastic and dredge the whole jelly in sugar, coating it evenly. Using a sharp knife sprayed with nonstick baking spray, cut the jelly into small squares (½ inch to 1 inch). Roll the cut candies in the sugar to coat the cut edges and place them in a single layer on parchment paper.

7. Let sit, uncovered, at room temperature for 24 to 48 hours, until the sugar crystalizes. Store in an airtight container at room temperature for up to 3 weeks.

Variation tip: Make any flavor/color you like—or pour the gelatin mixture into several different containers and flavor/color them individually. For instance, you might make red candies with cinnamon flavoring for consistency, green with mint flavoring, or yellow with lemon flavoring.

MEXICAN COCONUT CANDY SQUARES

⸺ Makes 64 (1-inch) candies ⸺

This pink-and-white layered candy looks so tempting in glass jars on the counters at the Mexican markets around where I live. The tasty sweet-and-coconut combination is not complex, but it is sometimes just what I'm craving after a Mexican meal. It's also very pretty wrapped in cellophane and given as gifts.

PREP TIME: **10 minutes**

CHILLING TIME: **1 hour**

EQUIPMENT: **8-inch square baking pan**

2 egg whites, lightly beaten

2 cups powdered sugar

1 cup shredded, unsweetened coconut

½ teaspoon vanilla extract

1 cup coconut oil

Red or pink food coloring,
    for coloring the candies

1. Line an 8-inch square baking pan with parchment paper.

2. In a medium bowl, stir together the beaten egg whites, powdered sugar, shredded coconut, and vanilla.

3. In a small saucepan set over low heat, melt the coconut oil. Stir the melted coconut oil into the sugar-and-coconut mixture. Transfer half the mixture to the prepared pan, pressing it down and smoothing the top into an even layer.

4. Add a few drops of food coloring to the remaining mixture and stir to blend the color. Pour the pink mixture on top of the mixture in the pan and press down, smoothing the top. Refrigerate for at least 1 hour until completely set.

5. Cut into 1-inch squares to serve.

Make-ahead tip: This candy can be made ahead and stored, in an airtight container at room temperature, for up to 3 weeks.

CANDY-COATED POPCORN

Makes 10 cups

With just 5 minutes of prep and 5 minutes of cooking, you can
turn plain popcorn into a sweet, colorful treat. You do need to let it
cool for 30 minutes, which will be, by far, the most difficult part.

PREP TIME: **5 minutes**
COOKING TIME: **5 minutes**
SETTING TIME: **30 minutes**
EQUIPMENT: **Medium saucepan**

10 cups popped popcorn (from about
⅔ cup kernels) or 1 to 2 bags
microwave popcorn
½ cup (1 stick) unsalted butter
⅔ cup sugar
⅓ cup corn syrup
1 teaspoon vanilla extract
Food coloring (optional)

1. Place the popcorn in a large bowl and
set aside.

2. In a medium saucepan set over medium
heat, stir together the butter, sugar, corn
syrup, and vanilla until the butter and sugar
completely dissolve. Bring to a boil. Remove
from the heat and stir in the food coloring
(if using).

3. Pour the mixture over the popcorn and toss
to coat well. Let cool for about 30 minutes.
Serve immediately or store in an airtight container at room temperature for up to 1 week.

Variation tip: Divide the sugar mixture into
batches before adding the coloring so you
can use multiple colors. Mix the colored
sugar with the popcorn in separate batches,
keeping them separate until cooled.

RAINBOW ROCK CANDY

⁘— Makes about 30 pieces —⁘

Rock candy is really just sugar and water, but it looks magical dyed with bright food coloring. Kids are always mesmerized by it. You can also add just about any flavor you like using flavoring oils or extracts.

PREP TIME: **5 minutes**
COOK TIME: **30 minutes**
EQUIPMENT: **Baking sheet, candy thermometer (recommended, but not required)**

Nonstick baking spray
2 cups sugar
½ cup light corn syrup
½ teaspoon flavoring oil of your choice
Food coloring, for coloring the candies
Powdered sugar, for dusting

1. Coat a baking sheet with nonstick baking spray.

2. In a large saucepan set over medium-high heat, stir together the sugar, corn syrup, and ½ cup water. Bring to a boil. Cook for 20 to 30 minutes. If using a candy thermometer, cook the mixture until it reaches 300°F. If you are not using a candy thermometer, test the temperature by dropping a teaspoon or so of the mixture into a glass of ice water. When it is up to temperature, it will harden and become crunchy immediately.

3. Remove the pan from the heat and add the flavoring oil and food coloring as desired. You can split this mixture into batches and add different flavors and colors to each batch if desired.

4. Transfer the hot mixture to the prepared sheet and let it spread into an even layer. Let cool for about 30 minutes until hardened.

5. Remove the candy sheet from the pan and dust it with powdered sugar. Break the candy into pieces. Store in an airtight container at room temperature for up to 1 month.

Ingredient tip: You can use flavor extracts in place of the flavoring oil, but you'll need to increase the quantity at a 4 to 1 ratio (e.g., ½ teaspoon of oil is equal to 2 teaspoons of extract).

CHOCOLATE-DIPPED S'MORES MARSHMALLOW BONBONS

Makes about 40 pieces

These fancy-looking, chocolate-dipped marshmallows are incredibly fun to serve for a party. Plus, you get all the delicious flavor of s'mores without having to encounter the wilderness.

PREP TIME: **20 minutes**
CHILLING TIME: **30 minutes**
EQUIPMENT: **Large rimmed baking sheet, skewer**

40 marshmallows
12 ounces semisweet chocolate, chopped
2 tablespoons coconut oil
1½ cups finely crushed graham cracker crumbs

1. Cover a large rimmed baking sheet with parchment paper.

2. Arrange the marshmallows on the prepared baking sheet in a single layer and place in the freezer while you prepare the coatings.

3. In a medium microwave-safe bowl, combine the chocolate and coconut oil. Microwave at 50 percent power, in 30-second intervals, stirring in between, until the chocolate is completely melted and the mixture is smooth.

4. Place the graham cracker crumbs in a wide, shallow bowl for dipping.

5. Use a skewer or toothpick to spear one of the chilled marshmallows and dip it first in the chocolate mixture to coat well and then in the graham cracker crumbs. Once coated, slide the marshmallow off the skewer and back onto the parchment-covered sheet, using a fork, if needed, to slide it off the skewer without disturbing the coating.

6. Refrigerate for about 30 minutes until the chocolate is completely set.

Substitution tip: Use any coatings you like. Substitute milk or white chocolate for the semisweet, and substitute shredded coconut, finely chopped nuts, crushed candy canes, or any other ingredients you like for the graham cracker crumbs.

DARK CHOCOLATE, CHERRY, AND HAZELNUT BARK

─── Serves 12 ───

Chocolate bark is one of the simplest desserts to make—it's just a matter of melting chocolate and sprinkling other ingredients on top. The fun is in getting creative with your toppings and making your own custom-designed candy bars. Any type of nut or dried fruit is bound to be a good addition, as are shredded coconut, bits of crushed candy canes, crunchy cereals, or broken cookie pieces.

PREP TIME: **5 minutes**
CHILLING TIME: **30 minutes**
EQUIPMENT: **Rimmed baking sheet**

12 ounces semisweet chocolate, chopped, or 1 (12-ounce) bag semisweet chocolate chips
1 cup toasted hazelnuts, chopped
½ cup dried cherries

1. Line a rimmed baking sheet with parchment paper.

2. Dump the chocolate into the prepared baking pan and spread it into an even layer. Place the pan in a cold oven and turn the heat to 350°F. Bake for 6 to 8 minutes, until the chocolate is soft and mostly melted.

3. Remove from the oven and use a knife or a rubber spatula to swirl and spread the chocolate around, which will help it melt completely.

4. While the chocolate is still warm and melty, sprinkle the chopped hazelnuts and dried cherries over the top. Refrigerate for about 30 minutes until set.

5. To serve, remove from the refrigerator and break it into pieces. Store leftovers in a covered container at room temperature.

Technique tip: To toast the nuts, spread them in a single layer in a baking pan and toast in a preheated 350°F oven for 10 to 15 minutes, or until golden. To remove the skins, wrap the hot nuts in a clean kitchen towel and let them sit for a minute or two to steam; use the towel to rub the skins off.

S'MORES CHOCOLATE BARK

— Serves 12 —

S'mores are my favorite dessert, especially when cooked by a campfire in the woods. But for a more practical party-friendly dessert, S'mores Chocolate Bark is a fun, festive way to capture the flavor. It is perfect to serve for a kids' party or wrap it in pretty little packages to give as party favors.

PREP TIME: **15 minutes**
CHILLING TIME: **1 hour**
EQUIPMENT: **8-by-11-inch baking pan**

12 ounces milk chocolate, chopped, or 1 (12-ounce) bag milk chocolate chips
4 to 6 graham crackers, broken into small pieces
1 cup mini marshmallows
½ cup white chocolate chips
1 cup marshmallow cream

1. Line an 8-by-11-inch baking pan with parchment paper.

2. Put the milk chocolate into the prepared pan and spread it into an even layer. Place the pan in a cold oven and turn the heat to 350°F. Bake for 6 to 8 minutes until the chocolate is soft and mostly melted.

3. Remove from the oven and use a knife or a rubber spatula to swirl and spread the chocolate around, which will help it melt completely.

4. While the chocolate is still warm and melty, sprinkle the graham cracker pieces and marshmallows over the top. Refrigerate for about 30 minutes until set.

5. While the milk chocolate layer chills, in a medium microwave-safe bowl, microwave the white chocolate chips at 50 percent power, in 30-second intervals, stirring in between, until fully melted and smooth.

6. Add the marshmallow cream and microwave again at 50 percent power, in 30-second intervals, stirring in between, until the mixture is smooth. Immediately spread the marshmallow layer over the set chocolate layer. Refrigerate for about 30 minutes until completely set.

7. To serve, break the bark into pieces. Store refrigerated in a covered container.

Variation tip: Make these more "sandwich-like" by adding a second layer of melted chocolate on top of the marshmallow layer.

ROCKY ROAD CHOCOLATE CRUNCH BARS

Serves 12

This candy bar-like confection is made with just three ingredients and takes about five minutes to create. Pop it in the refrigerator to chill and half an hour later you could be snacking on your very own signature candy bar. Like the Dark Chocolate, Cherry, and Hazelnut Bark (page 154) and the S'mores Chocolate Bark (page 155), this is a fun dessert to make with kids. Let them get creative and add other ingredients to taste.

PREP TIME: **5 minutes**

CHILLING TIME: **30 minutes**

EQUIPMENT: **8-inch square baking pan**

24 ounces milk chocolate, chopped, or 2 (12-ounce) bags milk chocolate chips

2½ cups crisped rice cereal

1 cup mini marshmallows

1. Line an 8-inch square baking pan with parchment paper.

2. In a large microwave-safe bowl, microwave the chocolate at 50 percent power, in 30-second intervals, stirring in between, until fully melted and smooth.

3. Using a plastic spatula, gently fold the cereal and marshmallows into the chocolate. Transfer the mixture to the prepared pan and spread it into an even layer. Refrigerate for about 30 minutes until set.

4. Cut into bars and serve chilled or at room temperature.

Variation tip: Add just about anything you like to these simple bars. Raisins or dried cherries, walnuts or pecans, or even bits of caramel.

10-MINUTE
PEANUT BUTTER FUDGE

—— Makes about 32 bars ——

If I had to pick just one dessert flavor, of course, I'd pick chocolate. But if I could pick two, peanut butter would, without a doubt, be the second. This quick fudge recipe contains no chocolate. Instead, its flavor is pure peanut buttery goodness. Nut butter provides the delectable texture, and it's even easier—and quicker—to make than Swirled White and Dark Chocolate Fudge (page 158).

PREP TIME: **10 minutes**
CHILLING TIME: **3 hours**
EQUIPMENT: **8-inch square baking pan**

Nonstick baking spray
2 cups sugar
½ cup low-fat or whole milk
1 cup peanut butter (smooth or crunchy)
1 teaspoon vanilla extract

1. Coat an 8-inch square baking pan with nonstick baking spray.

2. In a medium saucepan set over medium-high heat, combine the sugar and milk. Bring to a boil. Let the mixture boil for about 3 minutes, stirring frequently, and lowering the heat if necessary to keep it from boiling over the side. Remove the pan from the heat.

3. Stir in the peanut butter until it is completely melted and the mixture is smooth.

4. Stir in the vanilla. Transfer the peanut butter mixture to the prepared pan and let cool. Refrigerate for about 3 hours until completely set.

5. To serve, slice into 1-by-2-inch bars. Store in an airtight container at room temperature for up to 1 week, or refrigerate for up to 1 month.

Substitution tip: Use any type of nut butter for this fudge. Try almond or hazelnut butter for an interesting flavor twist.

WHITE AND DARK CHOCOLATE FUDGE

Makes about 32 bars

Fudge isn't terribly difficult to make, but most recipes require, at a minimum, a candy thermometer. Not this one. Using mini marshmallows in the mix provides excellent fudgy flavor. The white chocolate swirls make it extra pretty, too. This is a great fudge to have around for chocolate emergencies, or to give as gifts.

PREP TIME: **20 minutes**

CHILLING TIME: **3 hours**

EQUIPMENT: **8-inch square baking pan**

Nonstick baking spray

3 cups mini marshmallows

2 cups sugar

1 cup heavy (whipping) cream

6 tablespoons (¾ stick) unsalted butter

Pinch salt

3 cups semisweet chocolate chips

1½ teaspoons vanilla extract

½ cup white chocolate chips

1. Line an 8-inch square baking pan with parchment paper and generously coat the parchment with nonstick baking spray.

2. In a medium saucepan set over medium heat, combine the marshmallows, sugar, cream, butter, and salt. Cook for about 5 minutes, stirring frequently, until the butter and marshmallows are mostly melted. Raise the heat to medium-high and bring the mixture to a boil. Cook for 5 minutes more, stirring occasionally. Remove the pan from the heat.

3. Stir in the semisweet chocolate chips and the vanilla. Continue to stir until the chocolate is fully melted and the mixture is smooth. Pour the hot mixture into the prepared pan.

4. In a small microwave-safe bowl, microwave the white chocolate chips at 50 percent power, in 30-second intervals, stirring in between, until fully melted and smooth. Drizzle the melted white chocolate into the dark chocolate mixture. Using the tip of a knife, a chopstick, or a skewer, swirl the two together. Let cool to room temperature.

5. Once the fudge cools, refrigerate for about 3 hours until completely set. Slice into 1-by-2-inch bars and serve.

Make-ahead tip: This fudge can be kept refrigerated for up to 1 month. Cut it into squares and separate the squares with parchment or wax paper, or use paper candy cups.

DARK CHOCOLATE TRUFFLES

Makes about 30 truffles

Chocolate truffles are sold in some of the finest high-end chocolate shops in the world, so making them at home might seem intimidating—but don't let that stop you. Their success relies more on the quality of ingredients than on skill or hard work. Choose a high-quality chocolate you love as your base and there's almost no way you can go wrong.

PREP TIME: **30 minutes**

CHILLING TIME: **2 hours**

EQUIPMENT: **Baking sheet**

12 ounces dark chocolate, chopped

3 tablespoons unsalted butter

⅓ cup heavy (whipping) cream

1 teaspoon vanilla extract

Coatings as desired, such as sweetened or unsweetened cocoa powder, decorating sugars, colored sprinkles, finely chopped nuts, or shredded coconut

1. In a large microwave-safe bowl, combine the dark chocolate, butter, and cream. Microwave at 50 percent power, in 30-second intervals, stirring in between, until the chocolate is fully melted and the mixture is smooth.

2. Whisk in the vanilla. Let the mixture cool to room temperature, cover with plastic wrap, and refrigerate for 2 hours.

3. Line the baking sheet with parchment paper.

4. With a small cookie scoop or a melon baller, scoop out balls of the chocolate. Gently roll the balls between your hands to smooth the edges. Place each ball on the prepared baking sheet once it is formed. Repeat until all the chocolate mixture has been used. You should get around 30 balls.

5. Place your desired coating(s) into shallow dishes and roll the balls in them to coat well. Return the coated balls to the baking sheet. Once all the balls are coated, refrigerate until ready to serve.

Technique tip: If your chocolate mixture becomes too firm to form balls, let it sit at room temperature for about 15 minutes until it is soft enough to scoop.

Measurement Conversion Chart

VOLUME EQUIVALENTS (LIQUID)

US STANDARD	US STANDARD (OUNCES)	METRIC (APPROXIMATE)
2 tablespoons	1 fl. oz.	30 mL
¼ cup	2 fl. oz.	60 mL
½ cup	4 fl. oz.	120 mL
1 cup	8 fl. oz.	240 mL
1½ cups	12 fl. oz.	355 mL
2 cups or 1 pint	16 fl. oz.	475 mL
4 cups or 1 quart	32 fl. oz.	1 L
1 gallon	128 fl. oz.	4 L

OVEN TEMPERATURES

FAHRENHEIT (F)	CELSIUS (C) (APPROXIMATE)
250°F	120°C
300°F	150°C
325°F	165°C
350°F	180°C
375°F	190°C
400°F	200°C
425°F	220°C
450°F	230°C

VOLUME EQUIVALENTS (DRY)

US STANDARD	METRIC (APPROXIMATE)
⅛ teaspoon	0.5 mL
¼ teaspoon	1 mL
½ teaspoon	2 mL
¾ teaspoon	4 mL
1 teaspoon	5 mL
1 tablespoon	15 mL
¼ cup	59 mL
⅓ cup	79 mL
½ cup	118 mL
⅔ cup	156 mL
¾ cup	177 mL
1 cup	235 mL
2 cups or 1 pint	475 mL
3 cups	700 mL
4 cups or 1 quart	1 L

WEIGHT EQUIVALENTS

US STANDARD	METRIC (APPROXIMATE)
½ ounce	15 g
1 ounce	30 g
2 ounces	60 g
4 ounces	115 g
8 ounces	225 g
12 ounces	340 g
16 ounces or 1 pound	455 g

Recipe Index

Index

Acknowledgments

As always, I am thankful for my husband, Doug Reil, for his support and good humor as I develop recipes for dishes he cannot eat. Thanks, also, to my son, Cashel, for being a superior dessert taste tester. I am grateful to the team at Callisto Media including, but not limited to, Andrew Yackira, Kim Suarez, and Talia Platz.

About the Author

Robin Donovan is a food writer, recipe developer, and author of numerous cookbooks, including the bestselling *Campfire Cuisine*, *The Homemade Ice Cream Recipe Book*, and *The Camp Dutch Oven Cookbook*. She lives in Berkeley, California, and blogs about super-easy recipes for surprisingly delicious meals at www.TwoLazyGourmets.com.